Green Smoothies

by Bo Rinaldi

ALPHA

A member of Penguin Group (USA) Inc.

ALPHA BOOKS

Published by the Penguin Group

Penguin Group (USA) Inc., 375 Hudson Street, New York, New York 10014, USA • Penguin Group (Canada), 90 Eglinton Avenue East, Suite 700, Toronto, Ontario M4P 2Y3, Canada (a division of Pearson Penguin Canada Inc.) • Penguin Books Ltd., 80 Strand, London WC2R 0RL, England • Penguin Ireland, 25 St. Stephen's Green, Dublin 2, Ireland (a division of Penguin Books Ltd.) • Penguin Group (Australia), 250 Camberwell Road, Camberwell, Victoria 3124, Australia (a division of Pearson Australia Group Pty. Ltd.) • Penguin Books India Pvt. Ltd., 11 Community Centre, Panchsheel Park, New Delhi—110 017, India • Penguin Group (NZ), 67 Apollo Drive, Rosedale, North Shore, Auckland 1311, New Zealand (a division of Pearson New Zealand Ltd.) • Penguin Books (South Africa) (Pty.) Ltd., 24 Sturdee Avenue, Rosebank, Johannesburg 2196, South Africa • Penguin Books Ltd., Registered Offices: 80 Strand, London WC2R 0RL, England

Copyright © 2012 by Bo Rinaldi

International Standard Book Number: 978-1-61564-164-2
Library of Congress Catalog Card Number: 2011941053

14 13 12   8 7 6 5 4 3 2 1

Interpretation of the printing code: The rightmost number of the first series of numbers is the year of the book's printing; the rightmost number of the second series of numbers is the number of the book's printing. For example, a printing code of 12-1 shows that the first printing occurred in 2012.

Printed in the United States of America

Note: This publication contains the opinions and ideas of its author. It is intended to provide helpful and informative material on the subject matter covered. It is sold with the understanding that the author and publisher are not engaged in rendering professional services in the book. If the reader requires personal assistance or advice, a competent professional should be consulted.

The author and publisher specifically disclaim any responsibility for any liability, loss, or risk, personal or otherwise, which is incurred as a consequence, directly or indirectly, of the use and application of any of the contents of this book.

Most Alpha books are available at special quantity discounts for bulk purchases for sales promotions, premiums, fund-raising, or educational use. Special books, or book excerpts, can also be created to fit specific needs. For details, write: Special Markets, Alpha Books, 375 Hudson Street, New York, NY 10014.

Publisher: *Marie Butler-Knight*
Associate Publisher: *Mike Sanders*
Executive Managing Editor: *Billy Fields*
Senior Acquisitions Editor: *Brook Farling*
Senior Development Editor: *Christy Wagner*
Senior Production Editor: *Kayla Dugger*
Copy Editor: *Louise Lund*

Cover Designer: *Kurt Owens*
Book Designers: *William Thomas, Rebecca Batchelor*
Indexer: *Tonya Heard*
Layout: *Ayanna Lacey*
Senior Proofreader: *Laura Caddell*

Contents

Foreword

The Complete Idiot's Guide to Green Smoothies provides some of the best information regarding the easiest way to enjoy the natural and healing wonders of the plant kingdom. As a researcher and medical doctor in the field of health and nutrition, I provide information on a daily basis regarding the latest research on the subject. When you visit my website at nutritionfacts.org, one fact will stand out immediately: more and more research exists on the amazing qualities of the specific molecules only found in the plant kingdom and how these incredible compounds may help prevent, reverse, and even cure many of the modern diseases our world faces. If you wish to balance your blood sugar, lose weight, gain energy, improve digestion, or simply feel your best, a great way to start down the right path is by drinking green smoothies.

As a well-known health advocate in the natural foods arena, Bo Rinaldi has assembled hundreds of great ideas, facts, and suggestions we can all use on a daily basis. Bo knows this information firsthand, as his books, restaurants, websites, and cooking schools all focus on the plant-based lifestyle now being recognized as a great way to support our modern lifestyle in the healthiest way possible. Since Bo cured himself naturally of asthma and allergy back in 1960, he has been very active helping millions understand the natural cures a plant-based lifestyle provides when used in the way presented here.

Green smoothies contain powerful nutrition that heals and balances our bodies. We have found in the medical community that natural green smoothies can actually improve or cure digestive issues, diabetes, and obesity. This single fact could be what helps reverse the immense drain on our health-care system and reverses our current health-care crisis. I believe this is the easiest way to benefit from a plant-based meal for a variety of medical reasons, as the natural fiber, easily absorbed nutrition, and satisfying tastes show off the best natural food has to offer. A big payback while saving us money and time!

In the medical profession today, we are finally realizing that what we eat can actually affect us. When you make good food choices, you feel good—on many levels. The common diet of modern society has created myriad issues I believe we can reverse today and for generations to come. This book makes that easy, fun, and effective for everyone, from baby boomers to young children. Make a difference in your life, the lives of your loved ones, and all of society by using the wisdom, information, and ideas Bo Rinaldi presents in these pages.

"Go green for less green" is one of my favorite topics in this book, and sums it up well. Let's all take a step forward for our future and the health of our society by using this book daily and sharing it with all our friends, family, and even local physicians. I know they will all thank you.

Michael Greger, MD
NutritionFacts.org

Introduction

This book is a collective effort from a life-long journey that has brought me incredible health with many fascinating discoveries along the way. I have been a vegan since 1960, when a doctor, who was a Seventh-Day Adventist, gave my mother the book *Back to Eden*. At that time, I had severe, seemingly incurable asthma and allergies. Within 2 weeks of following the concepts in that book, I was cured, and I have followed the path of a plant-based lifestyle ever since— and that includes green smoothies.

You've probably heard about green smoothies, but you might not know what makes them so special. What's all the fuss about? The green smoothie is a style of blended drink that can include whole foods and juices, combined with any number of natural ingredients.

At the start of this project, I thought the idea of writing a green smoothies cookbook was both inspiring and daunting. With all the infinite varieties and styles of green smoothies, plus an array of ingredients so vast, I wanted to include my everyday favorites as well as the more exotic combinations that are special in their own right.

I grew up in Southern California in the 1950s, and I can tell you we all had our blenders whirring from the time we were kids. This set the stage for the organic health food boom of the 1960s, when we saw high-speed blenders able to liquefy just about anything. Today, with modern technology and science combining to bring us incredibly efficient appliances, just about anyone can blend green smoothies, the healthiest drinks on the planet.

In this book, I share the many options of this life-giving drink. I think you'll find the recipes delicious, easy to make, and most importantly extremely healthy. This book is different from many because on every recipe, I've included nutrition and scientific facts on every recipe.

In addition, I show you many of the secrets we in natural food restaurants and juice bars have been using for years so you, too, can be a master of these nutritional powerhouses. Flip through the following recipes—150 of them!—and find the smoothies that sound tasty to you. Give 'em a whirl, and soon, I hope you, too, will be a green smoothie junkie!

May this book answer all your questions and serve as a lifelong guide to your optimum health and well-being, all thanks to fresh, natural green smoothies.

How This Book Is Organized

I've written and organized this book to give you the most information about green smoothies I can in a way that's easy to understand.

Chapters 1 through 3 are designed to be the overall guide that will give you all you need to create the perfect green smoothie. After that, Chapters 4 through 11 offer you everything from everyday smoothies to smoothies for weight loss, and everything in between— including the increasingly popular superfood smoothies.

At the back of the book, I've also included two appendixes full of useful knowledge and information. First is a glossary of terms you might need to know, followed by extra resources to guide you in your quest for further knowledge of green smoothies and nutrition in general.

Extras

Throughout the book, I've included little nuggets of extra information. Here's what to look for:

> **FRESH FACT**
>
> In these sidebars, I've included tons of fun facts and bits of additional information.

> **TO YOUR HEALTH!**
>
> For tips on making your green smoothies tastier, more nutritious, or easier to whip up, check out these sidebars.

> **DEFINITION**
>
> Turn to these sidebars for definitions of ingredients, cooking terms, and other words you might not be familiar with.

> **BLENDER BLUNDER**
>
> These sidebars offer gentle warnings to help keep you on the right track.

Acknowledgments

Infinite gratitude to my literary agent, Marilyn Allen for guiding me in creating exciting best-selling books.

Big thanks to Beryl Greensea, who worked side by side with me on recipe creation and nutritional information. Beryl's real-life experiences in the natural foods, as well as raising a healthy family using green smoothies, adds a level of authenticity rarely found in books of this nature.

The amazing Dr. Michael Greger, Director of Animal Welfare at the U.S. Humane Society, has contributed countless hours to advancing the knowledge he discovers on a daily basis regarding the healing wonders of the plant kingdom. Dr. Greger, may the sun shine bright on you and your incredible works at nutritionfacts.org.

To the staff at the Blossoming Lotus Restaurant, we all appreciate your untiring commitment in creating the most amazing, award-winning, all-organic vegan dishes.

To Mark Reinfeld, one of my best friends ever and co-founder of Vegan Fusion and Blossoming Lotus (veganfusion.com), I thank you for being my muse, confidant, and spiritual brother.

To the love of my life, the brightest light I have ever known, Star Rinaldi. I was blessed the day I met you, and I am forever in your grace as your beauty and wisdom feed me the one ingredient we all need the most, love. It is my joy that you reversed many life-threatening diseases by following the concepts offered here and are now a vibrant lady who enjoys perfect health and vitality.

To you, the reader, from my heart to yours, thank you for letting me share this guide with you. May it inspire you and your family to create these fun, natural, and delicious drinks whenever you want to feel your best.

This book would not have been possible without the vision and creative energy of my acquisitions editor, Brook Farling. Thank you so much for allowing me to share my passion with all those interested in a sustainable and greener future for our planet. I have been able to touch thousands of individuals through websites, restaurants, speaking, and interviews, but the *Complete Idiot's Guide* series allows me to extend my reach even further into the homes and hearts of many. Thank you for your belief in me and my writings.

Trademarks

All terms mentioned in this book that are known to be or are suspected of being trademarks or service marks have been appropriately capitalized. Alpha Books and Penguin Group (USA) Inc. cannot attest to the accuracy of this information. Use of a term in this book should not be regarded as affecting the validity of any trademark or service mark.

Why Green Smoothies?

In This Chapter

- Powerful nutrition = a powerful body
- Green smoothies for healing and balance
- Improve or cure digestive issues with green smoothies

Living in our modernized world has changed household traditions regarding mealtimes. The dinner table has become a commodity, a convenient spot to toss the mail rather than a place the family gathers several times a day. People who are always on the go often skip meals and make poor food choices as a result of eating away from home. Fortunately, healthy green smoothies can restore balance to a poor diet lacking in nutrition and fiber. What's more, they're extremely easy to prepare and absolutely delicious!

In this chapter, we take a closer look at the myriad benefits green smoothies provide and the many valuable nutrients they bring your body.

The Ideal Meal

Smoothies are not a new concept. In fact, they're well established as an easy way to create healthy, great-tasting meals anyone can enjoy. When you think about drinking a smoothie, you might imagine a sweet, fruity, creamy beverage, but you can blend together many other healthy ingredients to create a delicious and nutritious drink.

So what makes the green smoothie different from the everyday smoothie encounter?

Green smoothies marry leafy greens with different combinations of fruits, vegetables, and healthy fats like almonds, hemp seeds, flax, and coconut. They're the perfect medium for turning in-season fruits and vegetables into a delicious, convenient, and cost-effective way to invest in your health.

Because green smoothies can include such a wide variety of produce, they have the potential to meet every one of your body's nutrition requirements—vitamins, minerals, healthy fats, and amino acids. What you get from one of these tasty blends is an easily digested, high-fiber meal loaded with potent nutrition and life-enhancing vitality. Green smoothies offer a rainbow of flavors and textures, and always make delicious, super-nutritious, whole-food meals.

TO YOUR HEALTH!

A heavier meal doesn't always mean a healthier one when it comes to nutrition. Even though many people eat calorie-rich meals to sustain their energy, it often has the opposite effect, taking hours to digest and providing little in the way of nutrition. Green smoothies are the perfect solution to eating "hearty" nutrient-rich and healthy meals while keeping your digestive system happy and free of toxins.

Good-for-you greens are possibly the most important food source for humans on the planet and could be set apart from other foods as their own food group because of how essential their specific arrangements of fiber, chlorophyll, and other nutrients are to your daily diet. But they're not exactly the tastiest ingredients. Luckily, green smoothies are like an artist's palate with endless ways to tantalize your taste buds.

It's almost too easy to create a green smoothie that will support any body type during any phase of life. In this book, you'll find recipes for green smoothies that provide sufficient calories to power you through your toughest workout as well as perfectly accompany any long-term weight-management program. You'll even find recipes that can convince the pickiest child to eat healthy food! Variety and great taste are the name of the game. The combinations are endless, and so are the health benefits!

The Perfect Meal for Busy Lifestyles

In today's world, people live their lives in motion. Fast-paced modern life leaves little time for people to sit down and enjoy every meal they eat. Eating on the go, at restaurants, at quick service outlets, or in the car is very commonplace, and this on-the-go eating style impacts not only the food choices we make but also the way we eat. Getting from work to workout while spending time with your family and keeping yourself on schedule limits the amount of time you can spend preparing and eating healthy food. Convenient, easy-to-make green smoothies truly are the optimal food for those on the go and are a great solution for our hectic daily lives.

Many products claim to be nutritious meal replacements, but unfortunately, they're anything but that. Sugary beverages filled with unhealthy fats, unnatural proteins, synthesized vitamins, and added minerals simply can't compare to the perfect balance of nutrients offered by fresh fruits and vegetables. Because they're loaded with nutrition, green smoothies really are the perfect meal replacement. In fact, drinking one may very well be the healthiest part of your day! So be sure to bring one along on your morning rush to work, and pack one in your child's school lunch bag.

Besides, it really is faster to toss some fresh produce into a blender and pour your green power smoothie into a travel mug or thermos than it is to make a complicated breakfast, and preparation takes little more time than making a bowl of cereal. Take advantage of the convenience that blending your own green smoothies can offer, and you'll save time in your busy day.

Chew On This!

Proper chewing habits are not something most people generally think about while eating. After all, we're generally more concerned with the way our food tastes and with satiating our hunger than the way we chew. But unchewed food remains largely undigested as it passes through the digestive track. This presents a problem when we don't absorb the nutrition we need from the food we eat. In the end, we eat more than we need and absorb less than the food has to offer. Regardless of how healthy your food choices are, if you're not digesting your meal properly and assimilating the nutrients, you're not getting the nutrition you need.

It's often a challenge just to find and eat our food before the end of a lunch break or in time to make it to class. Fully chewing food too often falls by the wayside in our haste to stay on schedule. After all, not many of us have the time to leisurely sit and chew each bite like our mothers taught us. However, blended foods offer essential nutrition in a fully absorbable state—and there's no need for chewing! Whether or not you're crunched for time, green smoothies could be the perfect solution to satisfying your hunger while getting the nutrition your body needs.

FRESH FACT

Chewing begins the digestive process by adding enzymes that break down carbohydrates. If you're drinking a lot of green smoothies, you might consider chewing on a piece of celery or pretend to chew your smoothie for just a moment to get your salivary enzymes going. This will ensure the most complete digestion.

Blending Is Brilliant

Why bother worrying about whether you're getting the most out of the food you eat when you can assure complete absorption simply by blending it?

Blending your food helps break down the particle size and provides access to more of the good stuff—the vitamins, minerals, and phytonutrients necessary for optimal health. The plants' cell walls, particularly leafy greens, are made up of insoluble and indigestible fibers like cellulose and pectin. Incomplete chewing won't break open these cell walls, and neither will digestive fluids. A salad eaten too quickly is a missed opportunity to absorb a great amount of life-enhancing nutrients. Blending your fruits, vegetables, and greens yields a much smaller particle size than even extensive chewing will. It completely breaks open nearly all the fibrous cell walls and creates the perfect format for those precious nutrients to be assimilated.

Because they're easy to prepare, green smoothies offer their optimized nutrition with the added benefit of minimal preparation time. Even the busiest person can spare a moment to clean some greens, chop an apple, add a few fresh veggies, and toss it all in a blender. Spending just these few minutes in your day to care for your health will reward you with great health and add years to your life!

What You Eat Empowers You

It might be cliché to say "You are what you eat," but there is certainly a great amount of truth to the statement. Perhaps it's more applicable to say that what you eat either empowers or hinders you.

If you eat foods that don't take much energy to digest and assimilate, you'll save your energy for the day's other tasks and activities. On the other hand, if you eat heavy, protein-rich and fatty foods, you'll expend tons of energy just trying to digest it and extract whatever small amount of nutrition it has to offer.

As an experiment, think about the foods you eat regularly, and try applying the qualities you notice about them to how your body feels. Are you eating something fried? Thick, greasy, sticky oil makes you feel the same way—slow and heavy. And what about a pastry made with refined flour and sugar? Does your skin look pale and pasty or overly dry? Maybe that muffin leaves you feeling dehydrated and exhausted from a sugar crash.

Now, take a look at a juicy cucumber, a bunch of kale, or some fresh strawberries. They're each full of color and nutrients. Fresh fruits and vegetables are vibrant and alive, and they impart these qualities to you when you eat them—or drink them!

Take note of the differences in the way you feel when you drink some of the green smoothies offered in this book as opposed to the other foods you eat regularly. You could even keep a log of the foods you eat for several days, noting the way you feel on those days. You'll surely see patterns emerge, and they'll likely steer you in the direction of more healthy green smoothies!

BLENDER BLUNDER

The standard American diet (SAD) is just that—sad. It's predominantly filled with nutritionally deficient white and brown foods that lack important nutrients and fiber. The life has been sucked out of our refined flours and sugars, and most of the vegetables we eat have the color cooked right out of them. Any color that permeates this brown and gray range is the result of artificial food additives. Gone are the outrageous orange hues of bell peppers, cherry tomatoes, and melons and the vibrant greens of kale and collards. Absent are the vivacious reds of beets and cherries, and it seems the deep purples of fresh grapes and blackberries are on the endangered species list.

Eat Real Food!

People get very caught up in diet misconceptions that demonize fats of all kinds and tout high-protein diets. It's just not that simple though. No one naturally occurring nutrient causes a health problem—or cures one!

The real culprit behind many health problems is our consumption of unnatural highly processed foodstuffs. Most of the fats we eat are heated to temperatures that alter the structure of the fat molecules and make them harmful to your health. The same goes for processed proteins and carbohydrates. A balanced diet is filled with the natural plant foods your body was designed to digest and contains a wide variety of naturally occurring nutrients, including proteins, fats, and carbohydrates. Remember, humans were healthier overall when they ate simple, predominantly plant-based diets, and although we currently have easy access to a wide variety of fruits and vegetables, sometimes it seems we eat less of them than we know is probably most healthy for us.

If you really want to experience superb health, pay attention to ingredient lists on premade foods, and don't eat things that obviously contain chemical additives or hydrogenated fats. Better yet, skip packaged food altogether and commit to eating at least half of every meal in the form of fresh vegetables, leafy greens, or fruits. You'll always get enough protein and will be consuming the amount of nutrients your body craves.

And the great news is that green smoothies make this process incredibly easy! If you commit to drinking one green smoothie every morning, you won't have to worry if you can't fit veggies into your lunch that day.

Instead of falling into diet fads and calorie-counting programs, just eat real food. Eat foods that are produced by nature, are unaltered, and need no preparation in order to be consumed. This is where nutrition is hiding, and it can be easily found when you blend a variety of plant foods into a potent green smoothie!

You Are Naturally Vibrant

A healthy body is vibrant, full of energy and life force, and feels good because it functions without major issues. For radiant health, it's important to consume vibrant, living plant foods, which meet your body's nutritional requirements without burdening it with stuff it doesn't need.

Just like a window in your house, your body is naturally clean and clear but can become covered with debris. Dirt impairs the function of a window the same way toxins disrupt the function of health and subdue the natural vibrancy, which are inherent to your body. A window is easy to clean though. You only have to remove the source of the debris obscuring its clarity to regain its intended function, and your body is equally as easy to restore to its original luster.

The important thing to remember is that your body is always striving to maintain balance and health. Finding the proper way to nourish it may seem difficult at times, but can be greatly simplified by drinking a green smoothie made with simple and natural ingredients. Vibrant, easy-to-digest plants encourage optimal health without complication because they provide balanced nutrition.

Optimally, the human body should maintain a *pH balance* that's about 7.2 to 7.8, which is slightly alkaline. An alkaline body with sufficient vitamins, minerals, and phytonutrients yields a clear, calm mind that can take on the world. The internal environment becomes resistant to disease and heals quickly from external injuries, it easily prevents or eradicates infection, and it fosters proper chemical balance in the brain. An alkaline system also regulates its cleansing processes easily, which helps maintain a healthy weight even in the absence of an adequate amount of daily exercise. When all the energy your body normally pours into balancing pH and avoiding toxic overload is freed up, you won't even find yourself reaching for coffee or sugary snacks to get through a mid-afternoon energy lull.

DEFINITION

pH refers to a scale used to measure the acidity or alkalinity of a solution. Water represents the number 7, which is neutral, whereas any number between 0 and 7 represents an acidic solution, and numbers between 7 and 14 are alkaline. **pH balance** refers to the proper pH of the fluids in the body, some of which should be slightly alkaline, to maintain optimal brain and body function.

We all associate having boundless energy with health and vitality, but too many of us turn to caffeinated beverages as a primary method of increasing energy. Such stimulants initially make us feel energized, but they leave us with more of an energy deficit than we started with.

Good nutrition is all you need to keep your energy up and your body moving. Take advantage of the best the modern world has to offer, and eat as many greens, fruits, and vegetables as you wish! You'll be rewarded with youthful and glowing skin, amazing energy, a clear mind, and a long life.

The Whole Body System

It's very easy to observe, simply by looking at the human body, that it is indeed an integrated and whole system. However, the world of modern medicine still adheres to the archaic notion that the human body is made up of separate systems that function independently of one another. This is a dangerous misconception and can lead to incomplete health care that focuses on treating symptoms rather than the causes of disease.

To care for your health or restore it from imbalances, you need to support every organ in your body. Your food choices are the first way you either help heal or damage your body, and certain foods are always ready to contribute their healing and building qualities to your ongoing needs for proper nutrition.

This is precisely why making healthy dietary choices holistically nurtures your health. Green smoothies are the most basic way to care for your body as a whole because they supply the complete nutrition offered by fruits, greens, and vegetables and still support healing and cleansing. With their organic acids and phytonutrients, they heal soft tissues like the skin and muscles, and with their ample vitamins and minerals, they keep your bones strong and your organs feeling their best. They regulate digestion and help keep blood pressure in a normal zone while lowering cholesterol and reducing the likelihood of onset for many diseases.

Drink green smoothies because they taste great. Drink them because they can supply you with the best nutrition. Or drink them because they improve digestion and allow your body to cleanse regularly. Regardless of whether you're drinking green smoothies to support a stressed-out digestive system or to supplement a restricted diet, if you choose to make them a part of your daily menu, green smoothies will support the health and longevity of your whole body.

The Importance of Colon Health

Emerging medical research is finally coming into agreement with the traditional wisdom that the health of the entire body can rely on the condition of the digestive system, particularly the colon. Just like the plumbing in your home, if the pipes get clogged, the sink backs up and you end up with a big mess on your hands. Keeping your colon clean and working efficiently is possibly the most important way to ensure your health.

Constipation is a precursor to many other diseases that simply can't take root without this first level of disorder. And this applies to both acute illness and chronic disease. Even mild constipation can be the deciding factor as to whether or not you'll come down with that cold that's going around. In fact, seeing a complete halt of symptoms after a colon hydrotherapy session is not uncommon, and many doctors recommend this method of treatment for even very young children who are prone to frequent illness.

FRESH FACT

Colon hydrotherapy is a method of cleansing the colon by inserting large or small amounts of water, which is then naturally released. This removes much of the plaque that can line the large intestine and prevent proper absorption of nutrients that normally occur in this part of the body. Colon hydrotherapy can either be self-administered in the form of an enema, which uses a relatively small amount of water, or it can be professionally performed in the form of a colonic, which includes a large volume of water.

If you're like most of us, the idea of colon hydrotherapy isn't exactly at the top of your to-do list. But fortunately, daily consumption of green smoothies gives you even better long-term benefits of a perfect digestive system than colon hydrotherapy ever could. Rather than getting a quick fix for a new or ongoing problem, you'll be removing the problem completely!

You don't have to succumb to the emotional and physical strain caused by digestive disorders! Just get on a regimen that includes a green smoothie in your diet every day, and you'll immediately begin helping your colon regain proper function so it can perform its very necessary job of keeping the rest of your body clean.

Ditch Your Digestive Issues

Today's standard American diet has created myriad digestive issues that were virtually unknown to previous generations. Colitis, Crohn's disease, irritable bowel syndrome (IBS), and heartburn are among the many increasingly common digestive disorders so many people live with.

Contrary to popular belief, the root of most digestive discomforts is a low production of hydrochloric acid in the stomach. If stomach acid isn't produced in the correct amounts at the proper time during digestion, much of the food you eat goes through the lower portion of your digestive system largely undigested, creating gas and disturbing digestive health. Undigested food then builds up as plaque on the intestinal lining, inhibiting proper functioning of the digestive tract and setting the stage for disease.

Processed foods, excessive gluten and proteins, and unhealthy fats are the main culprits behind these digestive disturbances. These heavy attributes of today's processed foods prevent complete digestion. They contribute to low production of hydrochloric acid and impair muscular movement throughout the entire digestive system, which can manifest as many different diseases.

Fortunately, eating lots of fresh leafy greens reverses these digestive problems. Their fiber restores movement to a paralyzed digestive tract and their chlorophyll helps detoxify lingering waste products that may already be making you feel sick.

It truly doesn't take much to get your digestive system and your health back on track; a bit of greens accompanied by some fresh fruits, vegetables, herbs, and spices will do the trick. In fact, cilantro, cabbage, parsley, fennel, and kale are all recognized digestive tonics. Each of these, and many other natural plant foods, contains active compounds that tone the whole digestive tract and help remove impacted waste that may be blocking the digestive system.

The Least You Need to Know

- Green smoothies make it easy to eat well on a busy schedule.
- Green smoothies empower you with vitality.
- Green smoothies keep your body functioning optimally.
- Drinking green smoothies can help you heal.

The Bountiful Benefits of Green Smoothies

In This Chapter

- Great-tasting fiber does a body good
- Essential macro- and micronutrients
- Good-for-you chlorophyll
- Super superfood and herbal green smoothies
- Saving "green" with green smoothies

The health benefits of regular green smoothie consumption are almost too numerous to name. But for starters, they provide ideal nutrition and support the body's normal cleansing processes. They're loaded with the micronutrients and phytonutrients that protect your organs and your entire body from degeneration and disease.

Chapter 1 touched on some of the overall benefits of green smoothies. Now let's dig a little deeper, nutrition-wise, to see how powerful green smoothies really are.

Fantastic Fiber

Fiber. You know you need it. And you probably know it's abundant in fruits and vegetables. But if the word *fiber* calls to mind gritty powders or cereals that taste like cardboard, you're in for a very pleasant surprise.

The truth is, green smoothies are the perfect solution to getting enough fiber in your diet—and you'll actually *enjoy* drinking them! They're so delicious, you won't think twice about the fiber content, but your body will surely notice when it gets a cleansing dose of the good stuff.

Have you ever wondered why something the human body can't even digest plays such an important role in maintaining a healthy weight and digestive system? Fiber is absolutely necessary for regulating your body's cleansing processes. Actually, the fact that it's indigestible is exactly what makes fiber work its magic. Rather than being absorbed by the body, it absorbs acids and impurities in the blood stream and colon. It basically sweeps the entire digestive tract, particularly the colon, cleaning your insides and stimulating *peristalsis* naturally. Drinking a fresh, whole-food green smoothie is like a spring cleaning for your digestive system!

 DEFINITION

Peristalsis is the natural wavelike motion that moves food through the digestive system. It's responsible for transporting food from the stomach to the small and large intestines and for the removal of the portions of food that aren't assimilated.

Imagine cleaning your entire home top to bottom and getting rid of everything you don't need. Your house immediately becomes more spacious and feels better to be in, doesn't it? The same happens in your body after drinking a green smoothie. It cleans your insides thoroughly and efficiently—like a sponge magically washing your whole house on its own. Without the extra clutter weighing you down, you'll soon feel lighter and naturally invigorated.

When your elimination system is running smoothly, your whole body works better because your detoxification channels are left wide open and ready to handle the amount of waste being removed from your blood and other organs on a daily basis.

Isn't it amazing that just drinking a green smoothie can have such a profound effect on the way you experience your body? This is the gift of the fiber in green smoothies!

Get Your Fill

Part of the reason overeating is so common these days is that readily available food choices simply don't supply the human body with the nutrition it needs. Even if your stomach is full, if your nutrition requirements haven't been met, your brain won't signal your body to stop eating. In its search for vitamins and minerals, your body will overeat until it finds what it needs for its daily functions. If your food choices provide more calories than dense nutrition, you'll likely be storing some amount of fat from the food you eat.

Of course, there are also those of us who eat for comfort rather than for hunger, and green smoothies will surely provide a safe haven for this type of overeating. One of the many wonderful benefits of green smoothies is that you can virtually drink as much as you like without worrying about gaining weight. If your belly seems like a bottomless pit, go ahead and drink another smoothie or two. You may even be surprised to find that green smoothies fill you up and satisfy you for far longer than you might expect.

Rather than filling up on calorie-rich foods, a common dieting trick is to eat calorie-restricted foods. Unfortunately, refined, highly processed foodstuffs loaded with chemical additives and *excitotoxin*-laden flavor enhancers are touted as the central pillar of weight-loss programs. Dieting this way compounds the malnutrition so many people experience today and does nothing to stop the drive to over-eat. By eating packaged diet food, you may be replacing some of your fat calories with protein, but you still aren't meeting your body's nutritional requirements. And you'll be eating foods that are very difficult to digest.

DEFINITION

Most marketed diet foods contain **excitotoxins,** or chemicals such as MSG, that are generally used for flavor enhancement. These types of chemicals overthrow the balance of chemicals in the brain. They are addictive and can be damaging to the brain to the point of killing brain cells. Diet foods that rely on these chemicals help people drop pounds by robbing their bodies of essential nutrition and end up doing more damage than good.

The good news is that green smoothies not only make eating healthy and dieting nutritious, they make it manageable and even pleasant! The ratio of essential vitamins and minerals to the negligible number of calories tips the scales in the favor of the dieter and the health food buff alike.

The Detoxification Aid

Detoxification is always occurring in your body to some degree. After your body utilizes nutrients from the food you consume, it must dispose of the unused food particles and waste products produced by digestion. Keeping your digestion optimized is absolutely imperative for these processes to properly take place. Without proper and complete elimination, undigested food can back up in your body. When the colon is impacted, much of the surface area becomes blocked, which prevents the absorption of nutrients and stifles healthy elimination. The waste products still need to be stored someplace, and this often occurs in your fat cells. Your body will retain water to buffer the toxic effects of these waste products as well as harmful chemicals and environmental pollutants.

Thanks to green smoothies, it's easy to get the fiber you need to cleanse your body and tone your digestive system, which contributes to an easier release of excess weight and toxins. In fact, fruits, vegetables, and greens, especially when grown organically, are all nutrifying and packed with lots of natural fiber. Many green smoothie lovers report fantastic health changes for the better when regularly consuming these nutrition powerhouses.

Nutrients You Might Not Know About

Green smoothies are incredibly rich in nutrients. They're abundant in the nutrients you're probably already familiar with, such as carbohydrates, protein, and fats. Plus, they're loaded with other, less-well-known nutrients. Most of these fall into the category of micronutrients.

Both macro- and micronutrients are essential to the health of your body. Green smoothies are the perfect way to ensure that you get enough of these energizing and healing nutrients without taking unnatural supplements.

Micro- Versus Macronutrients

Vitamins and trace minerals are considered micronutrients. Macronutrients, on the other hand, are the carbohydrates, proteins, and fats so often blamed for poor health. The latter are so abundant in the standard American diet that most dieters try to avoid one or more of them and reduce their overall consumption of each of these high-calorie nutrients.

> **TO YOUR HEALTH!**
>
> Each and every plant has a different ratio of carbohydrates, proteins, and fats. Likewise, each plant also contains a varied assortment of micronutrients such as vitamins, enzymes, and phytonutrients. This endless combination of nutrient factors is what makes a diverse diet so important. No one nutrient alone holds the key to perfect health, and none can be excluded from it. As long as you eat a variety of fruits, greens, nuts, seeds, and vegetables, you'll get the best nutrition possible!

Not all macronutrients are created equal though, and each has a rightful place in a healthy diet. Throughout the recipes in this book, the fats used are completely healthy and aid proper metabolism and nutrient uptake. The plant proteins are easily digested and readily absorbed without producing acidic results. And the sugars are metabolized slowly because they're naturally occurring and are more complex than refined sugars.

Fortunately, green smoothies are full of both macronutrients and vital micronutrients. However, fresh organic vegetables, fruits, and leafy greens contain many other vital nutrients including a range of phytonutrients, such as plant polyphenols, and enzymes only found in the vegetable kingdom.

Phytonutrients at a Glance

Phytonutrients are highly bioactive compounds found in plants and are especially concentrated in leafy greens, herbs, and the skins of fruits and vegetables. They often boast medicinal applications, making them essential to health and healing. These volatile compounds give plants their distinctive smells, colors, and tastes. For example, the pungent smell of thyme, the heat in chile peppers, and the dark purple color in many berries all indicate the presence of the phytonutrients classified as phenols. Likewise, the orange color of carrots and red pigment in tomatoes signify the presence of terpenes.

Specialty diets like the "grape cure" and "acai diet" are based on phytonutrient activity. However, these are incomplete and unbalanced approaches to health and weight loss because they focus on only one phytonutrient rather than the broad spectrum available from a variety of fruits, vegetables, and greens. Each of these bioactive compounds contributes to a successful health regimen. As a bonus, they're concentrated in green smoothies because blending a variety of whole, fresh foods optimizes the absorbability of these phytonutrients.

Every plant has a different set of valuable phytonutrients consisting of their various antioxidant-rich phenols, terpenes, chlorophyll, and organic acids, plus polysaccharides, organosulfurs, and enzymes, which are best consumed in their naturally occurring state. These fragile compounds need to be suspended in the living matrix of plant cells for proper absorption by the body. Phytonutrients support the daily functioning and repair of every organ, bone, and tissue in the body, and our bodies cannot properly function without them. Green smoothies preserve the integrity of these phytonutrients so you get the biggest nutritional bang for your buck.

A good indicator of phytochemical content is the color intensity in a fruit or vegetable. Usually, the darker the color, the more concentrated the phytochemicals. Thus eating dark leafy greens and brightly colored fruits supplies your body with a healthy dose of these healing compounds.

> **TO YOUR HEALTH!**
>
> We all regularly make color choices that represent us in some way. But while our lives are so full of rich color, our food is lacking. Color affects us; the colors we see affect our mood, vitality, and ability to heal. For example, red elevates the heart rate while blue encourages productivity and green calms and de-stresses. Yellow can be stimulating and even overwhelming in large amounts, while pinks and purples have a romantic air. The colors of our food do the same but in different ways. We cannot thrive without an entire rainbow of fruits and vegetables. The food pigments that give each juicy berry or ripe mango their distinctive colors also support our bodies.

Phenols and Terpenes

Some of the most powerful phytonutrient antioxidants are found in the color pigments in the phenol and terpene groups. The healing nature of these important micronutrients demonstrates exactly why eating a diet rich in fruits and vegetables can help treat numerous problems.

Under the phenol umbrella, we find dark blue and purple anthocyanidins, which are notable for their role in supporting the structure of collagen in the body's skin, muscles, and bones. They also protect the eyes from degeneration and scavenge free radicals caused by inflammation.

Also included in this group are more than 1,500 different bioflavonoids. Flavonoids are associated with vitamin C and together protect the integrity of the capillaries in the circulatory system. They're associated with a reduced risk of certain cancers, including breast cancer.

Flaxseeds are noted for their high phenol content of lignans, which display antioxidant, immunomodulating, antifungal, antibacterial, and antiviral activity.

Catechin is yet another phenol found only in the tea plant *camellia sinensis*. Catechin is useful for protection against prostate, breast, stomach, lung, colon, and skin cancers.

The colorless saponins found in beans, aloe, and quinoa belong to the terpene group and disrupt the growth of cancer cells. Tocotrienols and tocopherols are also colorless, and they inhibit cancer growth and improve cardiovascular health, respectively.

The colored varieties of terpenes include the orange, yellow, or red carotenoids such as beta-carotene, lutein, and lycopene. They also include the yellow and orange limonoids found in citrus. Carotenoids all are associated with protection from cancer and macular degeneration whereas limonoids offer general protection for the lungs.

 FRESH FACT

Phenols and terpenes are antitumor, antioxidant, antiseptic, and antifungal—all qualities that protect them as they grow. The transference of this protective chemical structure is not lost on those who eat brightly colored fruits and greens. In fact, many clinical trials confirm the benefits of consuming raw phytonutrient-rich fruits and vegetables and their application to many disease states.

Chlorophyll: The Secret to Optimum Health

Leafy greens contain copious amounts of chlorophyll. The benefits associated with consuming large amounts of chlorophyll are staggering. To begin with, chlorophyll is the ultimate whole-body purifier. Chlorophyll is essentially identical to the hemoglobin in human blood, which is responsible for carrying oxygen to the entire body. In other words, consuming chlorophyll oxygenates and rebuilds your blood, which in turn optimizes your body's ability to absorb nutrition and support proper pH balance. The alkalizing and oxygenating effects of chlorophyll encourage the expulsion of excess fat and waste products from the body.

This green-gold has also been found to neutralize cancer-causing free radicals, detoxify the body of drug residues and heavy metals, and regulate blood sugar. The antiseptic properties lend themselves to improving dental hygiene, infections, and skin disorders, plus the general anti-inflammatory properties make it useful for a host of inflammation-associated diseases. As an added benefit, chlorophyll is also a well-reputed body deodorizer because it cleanses the digestive tract, neutralizing gasses and acidic metabolic waste.

Polysaccharides

Although polysaccharides are largely colorless, they may indeed be pigmented by those colors that cannot be perceived by the naked eye. Polysaccharides are a basic component of energy-giving nutrients and also include indigestible plant fibers. These complex carbohydrates are the first energy source used when the body undertakes physical exertion. They're also healing aspects of plants that combat fatigue and stabilize blood sugar.

Fibers such as cellulose and pectin are also forms of polysaccharides. In particular, these fibers maintain digestive health and heal digestive disorders. Without sufficient fibrous polysaccharides, the body cannot regulate its cleansing processes.

Some polysaccharides like beta-glucan, found in mushrooms, activate the immune system. This particular compound also inhibits tumors and is beneficial for liver diseases. Beta-glucan demonstrates the ability to prevent infection, sepsis, and radiation poisoning and modulates cholesterol levels, making it beneficial for treating cardiovascular diseases.

Naturally Boost Your Immune System

The immune system is the body's mechanism for maintaining balance. People who eat foods rich in phytochemicals and other immuno-stimulating nutrients are noted with having healthy, glowing complexions that rival the luster of any suntan. As a whole, we're naturally attracted to healthy people with strong immune systems.

You might have already gleaned that green smoothies' nutrifying and detoxifying impact on the body also stimulates and supports the immune system. And rightfully so! After all, healthy food supports a healthy body and a strong immune system.

When dietary stressors are avoided and fresh, healthy foods make up the bulk of what we eat, the immune system just naturally becomes strong. Of course, we can all use an immune boost from time to time, and myriad superfoods and medicinal plants have their rightful place in supporting great health. Utilize your green smoothies as the perfect template to power up on some plant-based super immunity boosters!

> **BLENDER BLUNDER**
>
> When the cold season hits, don't be caught without a stock of helpful herbs and spices on hand. Browse through Chapters 7 and 8, and stock up on some ingredients so you don't have to drag yourself out into the cold … with a cold.

Superhero Superfoods

Superfoods are foods that contain high concentrations of life-enhancing phytonutrients as well as healthy fats, proteins, and balanced sugars. With these foods, you can eat even small amounts and still receive fantastic health benefits. Superfoods are the green smoothies' soul mate and the mainstay for amazingly vibrant health!

Possibly the most famous superfood is *theobroma cacao*, otherwise known as cocoa or chocolate. Yes, you chocoholics have reason to cheer! Cacao's mood-enhancing phenalathalamine and oxytocin give you that feel-good sensation that keeps you coming back for more antioxidant goodness. Many women intuitively crave the high magnesium content of cacao when menstruating because it rebuilds lost nutrients and relaxes the muscles that cause cramps. The best way to reap the benefits of cacao is to consume dark chocolate or even raw chocolate, made popular by the live food movement.

Goji berries are a small red berry native to Tibet and China. In this case, big things come in small packages. Goji berries are packed with 19 amino acids; 21 trace minerals; abundant B complex, E, and C vitamins; and essential fatty acids. Their beautiful red color is a good indicator that these berries contain more carotenoids than any other known plant.

Maca is a small root vegetable common to the Andes, where it's prepared and eaten like the potato. Known as a powerful adaptogen, maca is a general endocrine tonic. It restores vitality to stressed adrenal glands and balances hormones, regardless of the type of imbalance.

Chia seeds are the tiny, fiber-rich seeds of a plant from the mint family. Traditionally grown and eaten by the Mayan people of Central America, they're reputed as having enough nutrition to sustain you for an entire 24-hour period. Chia seeds are the number-one source for omega-3 fatty acids, and as an added benefit, they stabilize blood sugar.

Hemp seeds are often called the most complete food in the world. That may be a big claim to live up to, but if any food fits the description it's the humble hemp seed. They're rich in the proper ratios of omega fatty acids -3, -6, and -9 and are very protein rich. Hemp seeds are unique in that most of their protein content comes in the form of the simple globular protein structure, which is similar to the protein structure of human blood. That means it needs very little digestion to be absorbed. Because they are rich in most minerals and many vitamins, hemp seeds can easily correct common mineral deficiencies.

Also be on the lookout for the many superfood berries such as *golden berries, camu camu, acai,* and *maqui,* which all have important health benefits. Other superfood seeds and nuts include *flax, pumpkin, brazil nuts,* and *apricot kernels.* Add any of these potent superfoods to your favorite green smoothies, and you'll be set, nutrition-wise, for the day!

TO YOUR HEALTH!

For more great ideas on how to incorporate superfoods into your green smoothies, check out Chapter 5.

Common Tonic and Medicinal Herbs

Some of the easiest medicinal herbs to incorporate into green smoothies are also incredibly common. *Ginseng* is one well-known tonic herb and is used to increase overall vitality, strength, and endurance. Its steroidlike compounds can also be effective at treating asthma, insomnia, and depression.

Less-exotic herbs most certainly play key roles in health maintenance as well. *Oregano* and *thyme* can calm the symptoms of a cold and are also strongly antibacterial, antiseptic, and antioxidant. They both stimulate digestive fluids and calm an upset stomach.

Clove is antifungal and anesthetizing but also can be used for managing diabetes and may help prevent skin and lung cancer.

Cinnamon, like clove, is very helpful for diabetes management. It's an anti-inflammatory spice that calms most digestive disturbances.

Ginger, another amazing digestive tonic, is also linked with reducing inflammation. It dilates the capillaries, making it useful for circulatory stimulation, and has been shown to beneficially affect cholesterol levels. Ginger and its relative, *turmeric*, slow and prevent cancer cells from growing. In addition to being beneficial in the treatment of many types of cancer, turmeric is associated with liver detoxification, wound healing, and the treatment of inflammatory skin conditions.

While the number of beneficial herbs is seemingly endless, the ones described here are very easy to find and incorporate into green smoothies. Their healing qualities will boost your immunity and make the perfect addition to your healthy smoothies. In general, most herbs and spices have some sort of health applications, and it's wise (and delicious) to use a wide variety of them to support your ongoing good health.

Go Green for Less

Years ago, buying organic produce meant spending significantly more money than purchasing conventional produce. These days, the market has begun to turn in the favor of organic consumers, and most organic produce can be purchased for a similar, a small amount more, or occasionally a cheaper price when compared to conventional. It is manageable, even on a tight budget, to buy most, if not all, of your produce organic.

BLENDER BLUNDER

Conventional produce is a misnomer. In fact, organic produce is grown with far more conventional methods than commercially grown, mono-cropped, genetically modified, hybridized, pesticide-laden produce. You invest in your health, in the quality of the soil, and in the integrity of the entire food chain when you purchase organic.

Packaged, refined foods cost more than they appear to. They contain very little nutritional value, which means they don't satiate your appetite, and the flavor enhancers used in their processing encourage you to continue eating past your body's capacity to digest what you're eating. They're also very habit-forming due to the content of excitotoxins. Green smoothies, on the other hand, easily satisfy hunger and allow you to eat less while offering you superior nutrition.

Where you'll really save money, though, is on long-term medical care. When you invest in your health, you actually keep money in your pockets in the long run—and out of the doctor's golf club membership! By spending slightly more on healthy foods, you encounter far fewer and possibly no degenerative diseases or terminal illnesses until you're at a very advanced age. Your body will thank you in every way—and so will your wallet when your great health keeps the doctors at bay!

Drinking green smoothies every day really is a trade-up in your favor! You reap the benefits of a virtually disease-free life for years to come. So save your money for that much-needed vacation, and drink an exotic green smoothie when you get there!

The Least You Need to Know

- Fiber is essential to the health of your whole body.
- Micronutrients play an integral role in health maintenance, and they're easy to work into your diet with smoothies.
- Superfoods and herbs lend support to a healthy immune system and are delicious blended into smoothies.
- A green smoothie a day keeps the doctor (and the doctor's bills!) away—and keeps more money in your pocket.

Making the Perfect Green Smoothie

In This Chapter

- Great-tasting greens
- Avoiding blending mistakes
- Green smoothies for athletes
- Mixing kids and smoothies
- Easy nut milks and fresh juices

Are you sold on green smoothies yet? If you're not, you're about to be!

In this chapter, we delve deeper into the ins and outs of creating great-tasting and healthy green smoothies. Here, you learn many tricks of the trade, as well as how to choose a green smoothie recipe to support your specific nutrition needs.

Green Never Tasted So Good!

Let's face it. Some greens can taste pretty pungent and even bitter—especially, it seems, the ones that contain the most nutrients! Some people like bitter flavors and prefer them to sweet-tasting foods. For the rest of us though, it helps to blend such strong-tasting greens with ingredients that complement and tone down their bitterness. Both sweet and savory ingredients pair well with bitter greens and create a rich symphony for the palate.

> **FRESH FACT**
>
> Primates, our closest relatives within the animal kingdom, eat all kinds of fruits and leafy greens. Most monkeys and apes consume 75 to 99 percent of their food in the form of plants. And most of their non-plant-based fare is insects rather than meat. Apes, like gorillas and orangutans, have even been observed wrapping their fruits in green leaves before eating them. Looks like they got the idea behind the green smoothie before we did!

Naturally, when sweet dates, ripe pears, or fresh blueberries are combined with greens, the flavor combination takes on a new character. Combining a sweet mix like this with creamy hazelnuts or cashews will simply revolutionize all the ideas you may have about how greens taste. On the other hand, zesty lemon and mildly spicy, pungent ginger can turn your naked greens into a parade of flavor!

The best thing about the flavors of green smoothies is that they can be as different and varied as a chocolate milkshake and a fresh summer soup. Not only do green smoothies taste great, but they'll change your mind about eating naturally healthy greens in general. Don't be surprised if the highlight of your day soon becomes the time you drink your daily green smoothie.

A Few Do's and Don'ts

The smoothies in this book are all formulated for different purposes and supply different types of nutrients. Some are helpful for general health maintenance, while others are good for muscle-building and endurance. Still others are formulated for aiding in reversing symptoms of chronic diseases, and a few recipes have been created to make nutrition more exciting.

If you're brand new to the world of green smoothies, I suggest you start with the recipes in Chapters 4 or 10. More seasoned green smoothie connoisseurs might want to dive right in to Chapters 7 or 11. Whatever your desire, you'll find a recipe (or two or three!) you'll love in the following chapters.

Also keep in mind that these recipes are great guidelines, but some things may be altered to fit your personal preferences. For example, although ice isn't called for in these recipes, you may replace part or all of the water content in any smoothie with an equal amount of ice. Adding ice yields both texture and temperature variations you might like.

You should also feel free to use frozen fruit where fresh is called for if you prefer a thicker ice cream–like smoothie texture. Many of the smoothies in this book are served at room temperature because they're easiest to digest this way, but if you like your smoothies on the chilly side, simply add frozen fruit in place of fresh or use ice.

Accommodating Your Blender

In the recipe chapters, you'll notice I call for the use of a high-speed blender. This is an indispensible kitchen tool. If you don't have such a blender, you can still prepare the recipes in this book, but you must take extra care to ensure you're able to blend your smoothies thoroughly without burning out your blender's motor.

If you're using a standard blender, carefully layer your ingredients, beginning with fruits that are easiest to blend. For example, if you're making a smoothie with pears, apples, celery, water, and kale, blend the pears and water first until they're liquefied. Then add the diced apples and diced celery, and blend again. Finally, add the chopped kale to the blender, and blend again until completely smooth.

Fresh berries of all kinds are nice, small, juicy fruits to begin blending with, as is finely chopped cucumber. The basic idea is that you'll use soft and juicy fruits first and blend in stages until you add your greens at the end.

Go Organic!

Possibly the most important measure you can take to protect the integrity of your health is to purchase as much of your produce organic as possible. Commercially farmed produce can be sprayed with as many as 26 different chemicals per crop, and most, if not all, of them are known carcinogens. Many of these chemicals have very few tests performed to prove their safety before being introduced into our food system. And the tests that are run to measure their relative safety are performed by the companies who develop the chemicals to begin with!

On top of the health problems chemicals cause, consumers now have to be aware of genetically modified organisms (GMOs), which are entering the food stream on a regular basis. Again, the safety of such foods have not undergone sufficient testing to warrant their use, and significant data suggests GMOs are already causing adverse health reactions in humans and animals and are damaging our environment. As of this writing, GMOs have already been banned in at least 30 countries.

Of course, some foods are relatively safe to consume even if they aren't grown organically, although these change seasonally, so it's always good to double-check which foods are on the Dirty Dozen list and which are on the Clean Fifteen.

> **FRESH FACT**
>
> The Dirty Dozen is a rotating list of fruits and vegetables with the highest levels of pesticide residues that should be avoided. Currently the list includes apples, celery, strawberries, peaches, spinach, nectarines, grapes, sweet bell peppers, potatoes, blueberries, lettuce, and kale. The Clean Fifteen are foods with relatively low pesticide residues. They are onions, avocados, sweet corn, pineapple, mangoes, asparagus, sweet peas, kiwis, cabbage, eggplant, papaya, watermelon, broccoli, tomatoes, and sweet potatoes.

It's best to buy all your produce organic, as increased demand lowers prices, but if you simply can't afford it, then buy selectively based on the levels of pesticide residues left on your produce. Keep your list of fruits and vegetables that must be purchased organic current by checking the ever-changing lists.

Fueling the Athlete in You

Fitness buffs and serious athletes can reap extreme benefits from drinking green smoothies. In the recipe chapters, I give you smoothies that supply enough calories from complex carbohydrates, healthy fats, and easily digested protein to keep a professional triathlete on the run for an entire event! If you're a professional athlete, you can surely increase your performance ability by drinking green smoothies as a major source of calories and replenishment, which will help your body recover easily and keep your fitness in top form.

Even if you're not at such athletic levels and are happy with your amateur fitness enthusiast status, give one of these smoothies a try to keep your energy up and your blood pumping. Easily digested green smoothies won't weigh you down, and they'll inspire you to work out because of the extra energy you'll get from drinking them.

In addition to ample carbohydrates, fats, and protein, the key ingredients in green smoothies for athletic endurance supply abundant electrolytes and other minerals, necessary vitamins, fiber, and a host of soft tissue–repairing phytonutrients. Drink one green smoothie an hour before your workout to provide all the energy you need. After working out, try a healing green smoothie from Chapter 7 for mineral repletion and a speedy recovery.

TO YOUR HEALTH!

Sports drinks are an unbalanced way to replenish your electrolytes. Instead of filling your sports bottle with sugary, chemically created flavors and lab-manufactured electrolytes, blend a smoothie from Chapters 5 or 6 to keep your energy up and your body full of nutrient-rich hydration. You can also strain out the fiber from your smoothie to create your own vegetable-based sports drink!

Possibly the most important reason green smoothies are so perfectly indicated for optimal athletic performance is that they're very easily assimilated. Their liquefied nourishment takes the burden off your digestive system so you can redirect that energy into your workout. These alkalizing nutrition heavyweights are the real deal in clean energy!

Powerful Nutrition for a Powerful Body

You know you need to consume more calories when you lead an active life, but there's so much more to fueling your strength and endurance. Strenuous exercise increases the amount of metabolic wastes your body must remove. These wastes, such as lactic acid, make your muscles feel sore and burnt out unless they're removed from your tissues.

Fiber is one nutrient that helps remove lactic acid, but you'll benefit endlessly from the active enzymes found in green smoothies' fresh ingredients. Enzymes assist every process your body routinely performs for daily maintenance, so rather than drinking a stagnant protein drink, blend some active nutrition. You'll feel enlivened and have an incredible amount of energy and vitality.

Each muscle has only a certain number of cells, and muscle growth is not a result of gaining new ones. While muscles grow, tiny microtears occur in the cellular structure of muscle fibers. As they heal, your muscles become larger. This means you must accompany powerful workouts with much-needed rest. But remember that phytonutrients also play an important role in healing your soft tissues after a workout. In fact, many phytonutrients are essential to a full and speedy recovery from more intense workouts.

The dark purple and blue anthocyanidin in many berries offers integral structure support to collagen, which is the most abundant protein in the body. It makes up most of your skin, bones, and muscle sheaths and must be kept strong to support your active body.

The white pith on the inside surface of citrus peels and the little sacs that contain the juice are abundant sources of bioflavonoids, which strengthen capillaries and protect the circulatory system, so be sure to include them in any green smoothie that calls for citrus. Rather than using fresh orange, lemon, lime, or grapefruit juice, you may use the entire peeled fruit in your smoothies.

Drink at least one 2-cup green smoothie every day to keep your electrolytes balanced, your blood moving, your body healing, and your metabolism burning as part of your daily health plan. Your body will feel strong and healthy, and you'll have a glowing complexion that boasts of your great health!

What About Protein?

Many nutrition myths surround protein. But prepare to have them all busted, thanks to the wealth of nutrition housed in green smoothies. In fact, one thing you won't find lacking in completely plant-based green smoothies is protein! Plant foods supply ample amounts of clean-burning amino acids, and we've included tons of protein-packed ingredients in our recipes in Chapter 9, some of which contain more than 30 grams of protein in one 2-cup serving!

One of the biggest nutrition myths is based on what protein actually is. Proteins are made up of different combinations of *amino acids*, and millions of variations exist within the human body. Although the exact number of recognized protein combinations is debated, it's estimated that science has only identified what 2 to 10 percent of them actually do. That leaves a lot of room for controversy when it comes to nutrition, as in fact, every living cell contains protein!

DEFINITION

Amino acids are the building blocks of proteins, which are formed in linear chains made up of different combinations of them. All forms of life contain amino acids as well as other molecules. Twenty-two amino acids are commonly found in protein chains as well as many that are utilized by the body on their own.

Eight amino acids make up what's known as a complete protein, but it's a myth that sufficient quantities of these essential eight are found only in animal products. Yes, meat, eggs, and dairy products all contain protein, but they're lightweights compared to spinach, which supplies more protein per calorie than ground beef!

This is just one small example of where the myth starts. The rest of the story is most interesting, and the quality of different proteins and their respective digestibility is the most important knowledge you can have. Plant foods contain simple proteins that are easy for your body to break down and utilize for its nutritional needs. In order for your body to assimilate and use protein, it must be broken down first, and plants make this very easy.

The proteins found in animal products, however, are extremely difficult to digest, and after being cooked, they're even harder to break down and utilize. The body expends so much energy breaking down these proteins into amino acids that much of their nutritional value is rendered invaluable. In fact, current evidence-based nutrition on animal protein is beginning to show it's a root cause of many modern-day diseases.

Then there's the question of how much protein your body needs, as opposed to the recommended daily amounts. It seems intuitive that the time of life the body needs the highest amount of protein is during infancy because that's the most accelerated period of growth in the human lifecycle. But when we examine the amount of protein found in the perfect food for babies, the number is surprisingly low. Mother's milk only provides 4 percent of its calorie content from protein! Does that mean modern humans are overconsuming this abundant macronutrient?

Many health experts would say that not only do we consume more than enough protein, we consume so much of it that it's making us ill. Excess protein is not properly digested and eventually impairs the health of the whole body, according to many health experts.

Plants all have protein, and they have it in the amounts we need to function properly. I recommend that you turn your concern away from high protein content and look for the foods that offer the most nutrition. But if you feel like you need some extra protein for a heavy workout, just blend a green smoothie from Chapter 9!

Healthy Smoothies, Healthy Kids

It's of the utmost importance to demonstrate to children that healthy foods don't just taste good—they taste *great!* Their growing bodies are always hungry for nutrition (whether the kids admit it or not!), and any child who hasn't been exposed to addictive substances that confuse the taste palate will gravitate toward healthy foods if they are provided. Helping kids develop healthy eating habits can be challenging, so blend them a green smoothie from Chapter 10, and they'll understand that eating healthy can taste great, too!

Once you get their taste buds hooked on healthy, great-tasting green smoothies, they'll crave those artificial sugars and flavor enhancers less and less. And they'll be more attracted to healthier food choices—without any prompting from you! Don't be surprised if your kids start asking you for kale instead of potato chips!

Growing Up on Greens

If grass contains enough nutrition to supply a cow with all it needs to grow from infancy to adulthood, isn't it reasonable to assume humans could do the same? The answer is a resounding yes! Human children can be nourished in much the same way as our slow-moving, grass-eating friends, and they'll be healthier for it. Eating a variety of greens supplies your children with ample amounts of easily digested protein, essential fatty acids, and a full range of vitamins, minerals, and phytonutrients. Growing bodies need more nutrition per calorie consumed than fully matured adult bodies, so help your little ones develop an appreciation for leafy greens, especially by providing them healthy green smoothies.

While a child's brain is growing and developing, it needs abundant amounts of nutrients like choline, B vitamins, and omega fatty acids, among others. Growing bones have a continually increasing need for calcium and magnesium, and kids need to consume enough iron and easily digested protein to support their expanding soft tissues. Iron deficiencies can be very common in children in particular because not all forms of iron are easily absorbed. A healthy way to prevent or reverse an iron deficiency—and many other deficiencies—is to consume lots of leafy greens!

Hungry for Nutrition

Diabetes and obesity are part of an increasing epidemic among children across the United States and worldwide. However, despite the fact that many children are consuming more than enough calories, they're still malnourished. As I discuss more in Chapter 5, a major contributing factor to overeating is the body's search for nutrition.

If requirements for vitamins, minerals, and other micronutrients aren't met, the body's hunger mechanism won't signal the body to stop eating. Even if there's an excess of food in the digestive system, the body will continue to send hunger signals until it receives the nutrition it needs.

> **TO YOUR HEALTH!**
>
> Serving green smoothies to your children is a great way to ensure their health on every level. Aside from their ability to completely nourish growing bodies, green smoothies also help diminish symptoms of acute and chronic illnesses of all kinds! Keep your kids healthy through the flu season this year by giving them a green smoothie daily.

Fruits, vegetables, leafy greens, seeds and nuts, and various superfoods have the enzymes, phytonutrients, vitamins, minerals, essential fatty acids, and other nutrients that contribute to healthy bodies and healthy minds. Diets low in refined sugars and other processed ingredients that include whole, natural foods are associated with a low incidence of many health problems in both adults and children. Allergies, behavioral disorders, and many degenerative diseases are largely the result of poor food choices, but there are lots of ways to transition everyone in the family to a healthy diet or boost an already adequate one.

Setting the Trend for Healthy Eating

Dietary habits are largely formed throughout childhood and adolescence. It helps to get an early start with healthy foods, but it's *never* too late to start introducing new healthy foods! At the same time, even if your family maintains a healthy diet, green smoothies are a natural and worthwhile addition to your child's daily menu.

Fortunately, children are instinctive eaters. They know when to eat large amounts of food and when to fast for a day to help their bodies stay in balance. Most children love to eat a wide variety of fresh or lightly steamed fruits and vegetables if they're given access to them. Take advantage of this natural tendency, and feed your little ones as many foods from the plant kingdom as they'll eat.

Children who consistently eat healthy foods are far more likely to develop healthy dietary habits as adults. Having a foundation for good nutrition empowers kids to take responsibility for their own health and wellness as they grow. But even if your child chooses at some point to eat less-than-healthy foods, they'll be sensitive to toxic overload, making it unlikely for them to overeat junk food. And if they do get to a point where their chosen diet is making them feel unwell, they'll know exactly what to do to reverse it.

Because green smoothies are a highly nutritional food source, regular consumption of them may really help smooth the ride through the teenage years' roller coaster of hormones and emotions. A properly fed, alkaline body and brain aren't as susceptible to the chemical imbalances that contribute to depression and behavioral disorders that often occur in adolescence and beyond.

Regardless of age, adults and children alike will find that being properly supplied with vital nutrition diminishes the effects of daily stress on their minds and bodies.

Having Fun Making Smoothies

Preparing smoothies can be a bonding experience for parents and children. Smoothies take minimal preparation, so it's safe to allow even very young children to help in the process—as long as they're always closely supervised when knives and appliances are around.

If you don't mind a little mess, you can let the kids break bananas into small chunks to throw into the blender or toss in handfuls of berries. Have them tear up kale leaves, and let them scoop superfoods, too!

The simple act of blending a smoothie can be a wonderful experience of color exploration. Try blending them in stages so you can watch the colors change together. Start by blending an ingredient like vibrant red strawberries, add raw cacao powder if it's part of the recipe, blend again, and finally add your greens and watch as the color changes yet again! It'll be a different kind of rainbow!

Many kids will enjoy venturing out on a nature walk around the backyard or local park to find safe and edible plants to pick and add to smoothies. Many wild greens are mild-tasting, easy to identify, and grow like weeds. Identifying, picking, and eating their own food can help kids foster a love of nature and establish a healthy relationship with food that will last a lifetime.

BLENDER BLUNDER

Don't let your kids pick just any plant, and be sure to identify the plant as safe to eat.

Expanding Your Repertoire

Chapter 11 calls for many uncommon and potentially unfamiliar ingredients that aren't always carried at most grocery stores. These ingredients aren't as elusive or hard to find as they used to be, and you might enjoy discovering them in the specialty markets and health food stores that carry them.

The world is becoming such an ethnic melting pot, Asian, Indian, Middle Eastern, and Latin markets are very easy to find in many large cities and in most large rural communities. Each of these international markets carries a variety of produce native to their respective countries of origin. If you haven't done so already, go out and explore what your local international markets have to offer.

When trying new fruits you're not familiar with, it can be difficult to tell whether they're ripe. Don't take chances on blending unripe fruits into your smoothies because this may give you an unjust dislike of them. Always smell a fruit before consumption. If it has little to no smell to it, it's unripe. You may also enlist the help of a grocer or a friend with exotic fruit knowledge to help you. I sometimes use the pressure principle, which says that if you make a small imprint easily when you press a fruit with your thumb, the fruit is ripe. If it's too soft, it's possibly over-ripe. Take your time to learn how to choose fresh fruits for your smoothie, and let your experience be your guide.

If you're unfamiliar with any ingredient in this book, consult the glossary for a description of the look and taste of these exotic fruits and vegetables as well as where to find them.

With a little experimentation and creativity, you'll expand your knowledge of other countries, find new and exciting flavors to include in your green smoothies, and diversify your nutrition, too!

Fantastic Fresh Juice

You may notice that fresh vegetable or fruit juices are used in some of the recipes. If you don't own a juicer, you may also make a fresh juice by puréeing fruits or vegetables in a blender with enough water to get it to blend until smooth. Then, strain the purée, and you'll have fresh juice! The exception to this process is wheatgrass juice, which you may have to purchase from your local health food store or juice bar.

If you prefer, you may also skip this step entirely and include the added fiber of the whole fruit or vegetable in your smoothie. The juices are used here mainly to create a pleasing texture, but it's not absolutely necessary to use juice.

Nutty for Nut Milks

Many recipes in this book call for nut milks of various types. You may see a recipe for almond milk, Brazil nut milk, or cashew milk, depending on the recipe. Nut milks are included as a healthy, cholesterol-free alternative to dairy milks for creating a creamy-textured smoothie.

Nut milks are very easy to create and don't require any fancy equipment. All you really need is a blender and a fine strainer. You may use a fine mesh screen if nothing finer is available, but a cheesecloth, an unused organic prefold diaper cloth, an organic cotton gauze cloth, a paint straining bag from a hardware store, or a nut milk bag purchased online are all preferable options for straining the pulp from your nut milk. (The same goes for straining your fresh juice.)

Using one of these strainers yields a fine, silky-textured milk free of gritty, unbroken-down nut particles.

Following is a general recipe that may be used for creating milk from any type of nut.

Easy Nut Milk

This versatile recipe yields a creamy, delicious nut milk that's ready to be blended into your green smoothies! It is unsweetened to avoid off-balancing the smoothie recipes.

Yield:	Prep time:	Serving size:
about 2 cups	10 minutes	1 cup

Each serving has:		
454 calories	57 g carbohydrate	21 g fat
13 g fiber	20 g protein	

⅔ cup nuts of choice   2 cups water

1. In a high-speed blender, combine nuts and water.

2. Blend until completely smooth.

3. Line a container with cloth strainer, and pour blended nuts into container. Securing all edges from overflow, lift strainer and begin slowly squeezing and twisting the cloth, catching the nut milk in a cup or bowl. (Avoid squeezing so hard that the pulp bursts through the strainer.)

Now you have perfect nut milk to blend into your favorite green smoothie!

TO YOUR HEALTH!

If you find you prefer a richer nut milk, you can add more nuts, or use slightly less for a lower-fat nut milk. You also can soak your nuts for 1 to 8 hours to remove the enzyme inhibitors and soften the nuts for blending.

The Least You Need to Know

- Green smoothies taste great, thanks to the many wonderful combinations of sweet, savory, and even bitter flavors.
- Making the perfect green smoothie for every purpose is easy if you follow a few basic instructions.
- Athletes need balanced nutrition to function at optimal levels. Green smoothies can provide that.
- Protein can be acquired from virtually all plant foods, and the plant-based version is easier for your body to work with.
- Fresh greens are the perfect food for childhood nutritional requirements and help your child develop healthy habits early.
- Exotic ingredients offer diverse nutrition and are becoming easier to find, especially at international markets.
- Making fresh juices and nut milks for your smoothies is quick and easy.

A Variety of Everyday Smoothies

In This Chapter

- Getting—and staying—smoothie-inspired
- Green smoothies = nutrition quality control
- Creamy, smooth, sweet, savory, and more smoothie recipes

Drinking a green smoothie every day makes a world of difference in your health and well-being. It might just be one of the most important additions you can make to your diet! The wide variety of different-flavor smoothies in this chapter will keep boredom at bay while ensuring you get the right balance of nutrition and great taste.

Sure, you could buy a smoothie blended fresh at a local café or juice bar, or purchase bottled smoothies. But why bother, when you can blend your own supercharged green smoothies at home—and ensure the quality and nutrition they contain? This way you can be sure you're getting actual nutrition and not just a sugary drink. You can actually save time and money by using your own ingredients and making your own smoothies, and they will always contain more life force and nutrition.

The true benefit of drinking homemade green smoothies is the pure, vibrant energy you get from fresh fruits and vegetables. Bottled smoothies are pasteurized and are nutritionally defunct, sugary drinks in the guise of health food. Another problem with prepackaged smoothies is that it's impossible to guarantee the quality of the ingredients used. For quality control and uncompromised nutrition, take a moment to make your own fresh green smoothies every day!

Veggie Dill Smoothie

Fans of tomato and vegetable juice blends will love this smoothie. Tasty chard and pungent dill lend a classic flavor to a familiar drink.

Yield:	Prep time:	Serving size:
about 4 cups	15 minutes	2 cups
Each serving has:		
112 calories	24 g carbohydrate	2 g fat
8 g fiber	7 g protein	

2½ cups chopped tomato

2 cups chopped celery

2 large chard leaves

1 cup fresh dill

½ cup fresh parsley

½ cup water

1. In a high-speed blender, combine tomato, celery, chard leaves, dill, parsley, and water.

2. Blend until completely smooth.

Variation: Add ⅛ cup fresh lemon juice and 2 tablespoons minced jalapeño for an extra zing!

Blue Hazelnut Smoothie

Cabbage has never tasted so great! Sweet blueberries and creamy hazelnut mellow out the pungent flavor cabbage is famous for.

Yield:	Prep time:	Serving size:
about 4 cups	15 minutes	2 cups
Each serving has:		
541 calories	69 g carbohydrate	28 g fat
12 g fiber	10 g protein	

2 cups fresh or frozen blueberries

⅓ cup hazelnut butter

4 large pitted dates

1½ cups chopped cabbage

1 cup water

1. In a high-speed blender, combine blueberries, hazelnut butter, dates, cabbage, and water.

2. Blend until completely smooth.

Variation: For an extra dose of chlorophyll and omega fatty acids, replace the hazelnut butter with hemp seed butter.

BLENDER BLUNDER

Don't skip out on the natural healing effects of cabbage. There's a common misconception that raw cabbage causes excessive gas. Cooked cabbage can certainly make you feel a bit bloated, but raw cabbage is far less likely to be the culprit. However, if you do experience some gas, be aware that this can be a cleansing reaction and means that the cabbage is having a purifying effect on your colon.

Creamy Cantaloupe Smoothie

Blended cantaloupe has a creamy texture. Paired with spinach, it's sweet simplicity.

Yield:	Prep time:	Serving size:
about 4 cups	15 minutes	2 cups

Each serving has:		
131 calories	33 g carbohydrate	1 g fat
4 g fiber	4 g protein	

4 cups chopped cantaloupe   ½ cup water

3 cups fresh spinach

1. In a high-speed blender, combine cantaloupe, spinach, and water.

2. Blend until completely smooth.

Variation: You can use your favorite melon in place of cantaloupe for a distinctively different flavor.

Green Tomato Smoothie

This wonderfully fluffy and savory smoothie almost tastes like a light, raw, summer soup.

Yield:	Prep time:	Serving size:
about 4 cups	15 minutes	2 cups

Each serving has:		
150 calories	22 g carbohydrate	7 g fat
8 g fiber	5 g protein	

2 cups chopped tomato

2 cups chopped cucumber

⅓ cup avocado

⅛ cup fresh lemon juice

2 cups chopped dandelion greens

1. In a high-speed blender, combine tomato, cucumber, avocado, lemon juice, and dandelion greens.

2. Blend until completely smooth.

Variation: Adding 1 clove garlic, 1 teaspoon sea salt, and 2 tablespoons olive oil turns this smoothie into a great-tasting **Green Soup Smoothie!**

FRESH FACT

Common dandelion greens are not only nutritious, but they're reputedly healing as well. They're particularly indicated for liver conditions such as cirrhosis and are also cited as being helpful as an adjunct treatment for breast and lung tumors.

Fennel Fig Smoothie

This smoothie is like a Mediterranean dream. Sweet fig and fennel combined with creamy almond butter and tart lemon make a perfect companion to mildly sweet cabbage.

Yield:	Prep time:	Serving size:
about 4 cups	15 minutes	2 cups
Each serving has:		
445 calories	82 g carbohydrate	15 g fat
12 g fiber	7 g protein	

2 cups fresh figs	1 cup fresh fennel
⅛ cup fresh lemon juice	1 cup chopped cabbage
3 large pitted dates	½ cup water
⅓ cup almond butter	

1. In a high-speed blender, combine figs, lemon juice, dates, almond butter, fennel, cabbage, and water.

2. Blend until completely smooth.

Variation: This smoothie is also wonderful with 2 teaspoons orange zest. Use 1 cup dried figs in place of fresh, and use more water to consistency for an **Orange Fig Smoothie.**

TO YOUR HEALTH!

Fennel is a well-known folk remedy for indigestion and colic. It has an antispasmodic effect on the digestive system, making it helpful for gas pain. If you suffer from chronic or occasional digestive issues, make this smoothie a regular on your menu.

Cacao Cream Smoothie

If you're a fan of chocolate milkshakes, this smoothie is for you. Well, maybe it's not quite a milkshake, but it is as close as you will get with something this healthy!

Yield:	Prep time:	Serving size:
about 4 cups	15 minutes	2 cups

Each serving has:		
873 calories	90 g carbohydrate	52 g fat
16 g fiber	28 g protein	

1 large peeled and frozen banana

1 cup cashews

¼ cup raw cacao powder

2 large pitted dates

1½ cups water

2 cups chopped chicory greens

1. In a high-speed blender, combine banana, cashews, raw cacao powder, dates, water, and chicory greens.

2. Blend until completely smooth.

Variation: For a **Chocolate Chai Smoothie,** add 1 tablespoon ground cinnamon, 1 (1-inch) piece fresh peeled ginger, 1 pinch cardamom powder, and ⅛ teaspoon ground cloves. Try other greens such as dandelion greens in place of chicory, too.

Banana Chia Smoothie

Banana is a prominent flavor in this delightful green smoothie, and creamy almond butter brings it together in a fresh way.

Yield:	Prep time:	Serving size:
about 4 cups	15 minutes	2 cups
Each serving has:		
506 calories	58 g carbohydrate	30 g fat
12 g fiber	12 g protein	

2 large peeled and frozen bananas

⅓ cup almond butter

⅛ cup *chia seeds*

1 large pitted date

5 kale leaves, stems removed

1¾ cups water

1. In a high-speed blender, combine bananas, almond butter, chia seeds, date, kale leaves, and water.

2. Blend until completely smooth.

Variation: Adding ½ cup fresh or frozen blackberries brightens up this smoothie.

DEFINITION

Chia seeds come from a plant that belongs to the mint family, *Salvia hispanica*. These tiny seeds are rich in omega fatty acids, protein, and fiber, and because they gel when soaked, they double in size, making them great for satiating the appetite for several hours.

Clean Green Smoothie

If purity could be blended into a drink, this would be it. Just sweet apple and clean cucumber with mild kale.

Yield:	Prep time:	Serving size:
about 4 cups	15 minutes	2 cups
Each serving has:		
121 calories	29 g carbohydrate	1 g fat
5 g fiber	4 g protein	

2 cups chopped apple (your favorite)

2 cups chopped cucumber

4 kale leaves, stems removed

1 cup water

1. In a high-speed blender, combine apple, cucumber, kale leaves, and water.

2. Blend until completely smooth.

Variation: For a **Pleasant Pear Smoothie,** replace the apples in this recipe with pears and the kale with a wild, local, edible green.

TO YOUR HEALTH!

This green smoothie is a very simple recipe made with easy-to-find ingredients. It's also a perfect staple and default smoothie for when you just want to use what you have on hand. Once you get this recipe down, you can use it as a basic template to expand upon.

Mediterranean Garden Smoothie

The mild licorice taste of fennel melds wonderfully with smooth, sweet pear, and parsley enhances the refreshing elements of this cleansing smoothie.

Yield:	Prep time:	Serving size:
about 4 cups	15 minutes	2 cups

Each serving has:		
139 calories	34 g carbohydrate	1 g fat
10 g fiber	4 g protein	

2 cups chopped pear	2 cups chopped fresh parsley
2 cups chopped celery	⅔ cup water
1½ cups chopped fennel	

1. In a high-speed blender, combine pear, celery, fennel, parsley, and water.

2. Blend until completely smooth.

Variation: You can use ½ cup orange juice in place of the water and add 1 teaspoon orange zest for added flavor.

Blueberry Tart Smoothie

This smoothie presents the antioxidants of blueberries in a most delicious way. It's sweet and very creamy with a touch of tartness from the sorrel.

Yield:	Prep time:	Serving size:
about 4 cups	15 minutes	2 cups

Each serving has:		
537 calories	78 g carbohydrate	26 g fat
10 g fiber	10 g protein	

3 cups fresh or frozen blueberries	4 large pitted dates
⅓ cup almond butter	2 cups fresh sorrel
	1 cup water

1. In a high-speed blender, combine blueberries, almond butter, dates, sorrel, and water.

2. Blend until completely smooth.

Variation: Replace the blueberries in this recipe with raspberries to enhance the tart flavor of sorrel.

Green Gazpacho Smoothie

This light yet very savory smoothie has a bit of a kick to it. It's similar in flavor to a mild gazpacho.

Yield:	Prep time:	Serving size:
about 4 cups	15 minutes	2 cups

Each serving has:		
188 calories	15 g carbohydrate	14 g fat
5 g fiber	3 g protein	

2½ cups chopped tomato	½ cup water
2 cups celery	⅛ tsp. cayenne
2 cups fresh cilantro	2 TB. flaxseed oil

1. In a high-speed blender, combine tomato, celery, cilantro, water, cayenne, and flaxseed oil.

2. Blend until completely smooth.

Variation: Enhance this blend and create a **Savory Tomato Smoothie** by adding 1 teaspoon sea salt and ⅛ cup fresh lemon juice, making it more like a green soup.

 FRESH FACT

Cilantro may be a common seasoning and garnish, but did you know it's also a powerful heavy metal detoxifier? It also serves as a digestive aid and stimulates weight loss.

Sweet Lime Smoothie

Wherever this smoothie is, you will find summer. Juicy, sweet watermelon, sour lime, and pungent parsley evoke the flavor of a classic summer garden bounty.

Yield:	Prep time:	Serving size:
about 4 cups	15 minutes	2 cups
Each serving has:		
140 calories	36 g carbohydrate	1 g fat
3 g fiber	3 g protein	

4 cups chopped watermelon   1 cup chopped fresh parsley
½ cup fresh lime juice

1. In a high-speed blender, combine watermelon, lime juice, and parsley.

2. Blend until completely smooth.

Variation: To turn this smoothie into a cleansing powerhouse, add ⅓ cup filleted aloe vera.

FRESH FACT

Aloe vera is a succulent plant with long, fleshy leaves that have spines along the outer edges. To prepare aloe for your smoothie you must fillet it, or carefully cut away the tough skin of the plant. The result is a clear or slightly purplish translucent jelly ready to go into your smoothie. This is filleted aloe vera in its most healing form.

Lemon Drop Smoothie

This uncomplicated fruity blend is the perfect substitute for normally sugary and nutritionally depleted juice. It maintains its sweet flavor and attractive tropical zing while supplying you with great nutrition.

Yield:	Prep time:	Serving size:
about 4 cups	15 minutes	2 cups

Each serving has:		
272 calories	71 g carbohydrate	1 g fat
8 g fiber	3 g protein	

⅔ cup pineapple	½ cup chopped mango
½ cup fresh lemon juice	4 large pitted dates
½ cup fresh or frozen strawberries	4 kale leaves, stems removed
	1 cup water

1. In a high-speed blender, combine pineapple, lemon juice, strawberries, mango, dates, kale leaves, and water.

2. Blend until completely smooth.

Variation: Experiment with the flavors of this smoothie by omitting mango and substituting ½ cup pineapple instead. Or use more mango and omit pineapple.

BLENDER BLUNDER

Juices are a favorite among children, but store-bought pasteurized juice is high in sugar, low in vitamins, and devoid of enzymes. The concentrated sugars also erode tooth enamel and upset the pH of a healthy mouth. Instead of giving your kids low-nutrient processed juices, let your kids indulge in the sweet fruity goodness of this smoothie, which provides balanced nutrition and adds fiber to their diets. The chlorophyll from the greens even helps protect tooth enamel!

Blissful Berry Smoothie

Berries are the perfect way to get a tasty phytonutrient boost any time of the year. The sweet, complex berry flavor of this smoothie will have you buzzing each time you try it.

Yield:	Prep time:	Serving size:
about 4 cups	15 minutes	2 cups

Each serving has:		
479 calories	60 g carbohydrate	26 g fat
12 g fiber	14 g protein	

1 cup fresh or frozen strawberries

1 cup fresh or frozen blackberries

1 cup fresh or frozen blueberries

6 dried figs

½ cup cashews

1 tsp. vanilla extract

3 cups fresh spinach

1 cup water

1. In a high-speed blender, combine strawberries, blackberries, blueberries, figs, cashews, vanilla extract, spinach, and water.

2. Blend until completely smooth.

Variation: You may also add ¼ cup goji berries to this recipe or substitute any of the mentioned berries with more exotic varieties such as black raspberries.

Herb Garden Smoothie

This smoothie has a complex herbal flavor and just the right amount of sweetness to enhance the savory aspects of the herbs and sea salt.

Yield:	Prep time:	Serving size:
about 4 cups	15 minutes	2 cups

Each serving has:		
220 calories	25 g carbohydrate	14 g fat
6 g fiber	2 g protein	

1½ cups chopped pear

1 cup chopped celery

2 cups chopped chard leaves, stems removed

½ cup chopped fresh cilantro

¼ cup chopped fresh basil

¼ cup fresh mint leaves

1 tsp. fresh thyme leaves

⅛ cup fresh lemon juice

2 TB. flaxseed oil

½ tsp. sea salt

1½ cups water

1. In a high-speed blender, combine pear, celery, chard leaves, cilantro, basil, mint leaves, thyme leaves, lemon juice, flaxseed oil, sea salt, and water.

2. Blend until completely smooth.

Variation: Alternatively, replace the pear with equal amounts of apple, and replace the thyme with fresh lavender and rosemary to create a very special **Pear de Provence Smoothie.**

FRESH FACT

Fresh herbs contain bioactive compounds that make them taste and smell wonderful and add health benefits to your smoothies. Your neighborhood or even your own yard can be great sources for finding common herbs that will enhance your health and jazz up your green smoothies!

Powerful Superfood Smoothies

In This Chapter

- Introducing superfoods
- Tips for finding and choosing superfoods
- Sensational superfood smoothie recipes

Not many foods contain an abundance of hard-to-find vitamins, minerals, omega fatty acids, and phytonutrients. Those that do contain these nutrients in quantity are called *superfoods* because they're so packed with nutrition, consuming even small amounts of them meet your substantial nutritional requirements. Take advantage of these superfoods, and load up your green smoothies with these good-for-you ingredients. They'll elevate your nutrition and satisfy your body on many levels.

Most health food stores now carry a simple variety of superfoods such as raw cacao, chia seeds, maca, acai, and goji berries, but others can be purchased online if you can't find them at your local natural foods market. However, most retailers are open to carrying new items and appreciate customer input, so don't be shy about asking your grocer about some items they don't currently carry. (Also see Appendix B for a list of online resources that carry some of these harder-to-find ingredients.)

Amazon Berry Smoothie

Acai is a very mild-tasting berry that has hints of earthy vanilla. The sweet flavor and creamy texture of this smoothie are reminiscent of an exotic ice cream.

Yield:	Prep time:	Serving size:
about 4 cups	15 minutes	2 cups

Each serving has:		
430 calories	45 g carbohydrate	17 g fat
3 g fiber	4 g protein	

2 cups frozen, unsweetened acai

Water and meat of 1 young coconut

3 TB. maple syrup

2 cups fresh spinach

1. In a high-speed blender, combine acai, coconut water and meat, maple syrup, and spinach.

2. Blend until completely smooth.

TO YOUR HEALTH!

Frozen acai is becoming a standard item in the frozen section at most health food stores, but if yours doesn't carry it, you can purchase freeze-dried acai online. If you go this route, use 2 tablespoons acai powder and add water from a second coconut.

Nutty Maca Smoothie

This sweet and earthy smoothie has complex flavors of chocolate and malt and has a pleasant nuttiness that's enhanced by the creamy texture.

Yield:	Prep time:	Serving size:
about 4 cups	15 minutes	2 cups
Each serving has:		
364 calories	69 g carbohydrate	12 g fat
20 g fiber	10 g protein	

2 cups fresh almond milk	1 TB. maca powder
2 large peeled and frozen bananas	¼ cup carob powder
¼ cup lucuma powder	2 cups chopped chicory greens

1. In a high-speed blender, combine almond milk, bananas, lucuma powder, maca powder, carob powder, and chicory greens.

2. Blend until completely smooth.

Variation: If you're familiar with and like the pungent flavor of the tropical fruit durian, you can replace the banana and lucuma powder with 1½ cups seeded durian.

FRESH FACT

Maca is a unique food in that it supports and tones the entire endocrine system. It helps balance hormones, regardless of the imbalance. A person producing too much estrogen and a person producing too little can both use maca and be equally benefitted. It also supports stressed adrenal glands, making it useful as an adaptogen. Look for maca (and lucuma powder) in health food stores and online.

Spirulina Spiral Smoothie

This is sure to be a favorite smoothie for the whole family. Nutty almond butter, raw chocolate, and frozen banana yield a milkshake texture and make the perfect vehicle for potent spirulina.

Yield:	Prep time:	Serving size:
about 4 cups	15 minutes	2 cups

Each serving has:		
440 calories	77 g carbohydrate	28 g fat
15 g fiber	15 g protein	

2 large peeled and frozen bananas	⅓ cup almond butter
2 large pitted dates	¼ cup raw cacao powder
½ cup chopped celery	1 TB. spirulina
	1½ cups water

1. In a high-speed blender, combine bananas, dates, celery, almond butter, raw cacao powder, spirulina, and water.

2. Blend until completely smooth.

Variation: You can omit the spirulina and celery and replace them with 4 kale leaves if you like.

BLENDER BLUNDER

For some reason, spirulina and chocolate go well together. The one thing you should always avoid in combination with this algae, though, is any acidic ingredient. Citrus and spirulina just don't mix. Keep these two ingredients in their respective places.

Superberry Hemp Smoothie

A bold berry flavor is sweetened to perfection with dates and blended with rich hemp seeds in this *anthocyanin*-dense smoothie.

Yield:	Prep time:	Serving size:
about 4 cups	15 minutes	2 cups

Each serving has:		
648 calories	86 g carbohydrate	27 g fat
14 g fiber	26 g protein	

2 cups fresh or frozen blueberries

⅓ cup dried elderberries

½ cup frozen black raspberries

½ cup hemp seeds

5 large pitted dates

4 kale leaves, stems removed

½ cup water

1. In a high-speed blender, combine blueberries, elderberries, black raspberries, hemp seeds, dates, kale leaves, and water.

2. Blend until completely smooth.

Variation: If you don't have access to elderberries or black raspberries, turn this into a **Black Beauty Smoothie** by including 1 (100-gram) packet frozen acai and ½ cup frozen or fresh blackberries instead.

DEFINITION

Anthocyanins are the blue, purple, or red pigments in fruits, vegetables, and other plants and belong to the group of phytonutrients known as phenols. These pigments have shown promising benefits in treating cancer, inflammation, diabetes, bacterial infections, and a host of other afflictions.

Pineapple Tart Smoothie

The tropical, acidic flavor of ripe pineapple is perfectly complemented by tart Incan berries, sour camu camu, and slightly sour sorrel.

Yield:	Prep time:	Serving size:
about 4 cups	15 minutes	2 cups

Each serving has:		
328 calories	69 g carbohydrate	5 g fat
13 g fiber	6 g protein	

4 cups chopped pineapple

¼ cup Incan berries (also known as golden berries)

1 TB. camu camu powder

2 TB. chia seeds

2 cups fresh sorrel

½ cup water

1. In a high-speed blender, combine pineapple, Incan berries, camu camu powder, 1 tablespoon chia seeds, sorrel, and water.

2. Blend until completely smooth.

3. Add remaining 1 tablespoon chia seeds, and stir.

Variation: For a **Red Pineapple Smoothie,** replace the Incan berries with ¼ cup goji berries and the camu camu powder with 2 tablespoons fresh lemon juice.

Brazilian Chocolate Smoothie

This smoothie is the perfect replacement for chocolate milk. Mache is a very subtle-tasting green, allowing it to hide under the flavors of deep chocolate and sweet dates.

Yield:	Prep time:	Serving size:
about 4 cups	15 minutes	2 cups

Each serving has:		
960 calories	90 g carbohydrate	48 g fat
25 g fiber	27 g protein	

3 cups Brazil nut milk

5 large pitted dates

⅓ cup raw cacao powder

1 TB. maca powder

3 cups mache

1 TB. ground cinnamon

⅛ tsp. cayenne

1. In a high-speed blender, combine Brazil nut milk, dates, raw cacao powder, maca powder, mache, cinnamon, and cayenne.

2. Blend until completely smooth.

Variation: For a more traditional chocolate milk taste, you can leave out the cinnamon and cayenne.

FRESH FACT

Brazil nuts really are special among tree nuts. They're one of the best sources of the antioxidant trace mineral selenium, which is necessary for proper bodily functioning. Low levels of selenium leaves the body vulnerable to a host of diseases and creates complications for existing ones, so drink up! There are virtually no commercial Brazil nut farms, so these nuts are still hand-harvested in their native environment.

Liver Lovin' Smoothie

Sweet figs and goji berries mellow normally bitter dandelion.
Nutty and incredibly rich, creamy pine nuts make this liver-toning
smoothie delightful to the palate.

Yield:	Prep time:	Serving size:
about 4 cups	15 minutes	2 cups
Each serving has:		
460 calories	107 g carbohydrate	30 g fat
27 g fiber	13 g protein	

¼ cup chia seeds

¼ cup pine nuts

½ cup goji berries

⅔ cup dried figs

2 tsp. milk thistle powder

2 cups dandelion greens

3 cups water

1. In a high-speed blender, combine chia seeds, pine nuts, goji
   berries, figs, milk thistle powder, dandelion greens, and water.

2. Blend until completely smooth.

Variation: For a more potent liver-detoxifying effect, omit the pine
nuts.

TO YOUR HEALTH!

The bitter taste of some greens deter many people from trying them,
thus missing out on their benefits. Don't let bitter dandelion greens scare
you away from this sweet and balanced liver-tonifying smoothie. Give
your body some extra love and support and your taste buds a pleasant
adventure!

Powerful Pecan Smoothie

This creamy vanilla and pecan smoothie packs a powerful punch. Energizing maca and ginseng give your stamina an extra push.

Yield:	Prep time:	Serving size:
about 4 cups	15 minutes	2 cups
Each serving has:		
803 calories	70 g carbohydrate	52 g fat
13 g fiber	10 g protein	

¾ cup pecans

1 tsp. vanilla extract

6 large pitted dates

1 TB. maca powder

1 TB. ginseng powder

½ tsp. sea salt

4 kale leaves, stems removed

3 cups water

1. In a high-speed blender, combine pecans, vanilla extract, dates, maca powder, ginseng powder, sea salt, kale leaves, and water.

2. Blend until completely smooth.

Variation: Consider topping this power superfood smoothie with some hemp seeds for added protein and omegas.

Potent Pine Smoothie

Pine nuts and pine pollen combine wonderfully with the natural antioxidant power packed in this amazing smoothie.

Yield:	Prep time:	Serving size:
about 4 cups	15 minutes	2 cups
Each serving has:		
422 calories	46 g carbohydrate	26 g fat
9 g fiber	9 g protein	

⅓ cup pine nuts	2 cups carrot juice
1 TB. pine pollen	1 cup chopped celery
2 large pitted dates	⅛ cup wheatgrass juice
2 cups chopped cabbage	

1. In a high-speed blender, combine pine nuts, pine pollen, dates, cabbage, carrot juice, celery, and wheatgrass juice.

2. Blend until completely smooth.

Variation: If you prefer, you may substitute bee pollen for the pine pollen. It's easy to find at most health food stores.

FRESH FACT

Pine pollen really has too many benefits to name! It's a complete protein that's easily digested and is one of few food sources for DHEA, which is what fish oil supplements are generally utilized for. It has an impressive array of trace minerals like manganese and molybdenum as well as enzymes and hard-to-find nutrients like organic sulfur, which is needed for healthy body tissues. This hand-harvested pollen is tonifying to the entire body. Among its reputed benefits are the strengthening of the endocrine system, boosting the immune system, and regenerating liver cells. If you can't find it locally, buy it online.

Matcha Magic Smoothie

The slightly bitter flavor of green tea graces this smoothie with a nutrient-rich energy kick. This smoothie is green all the way but is sweet and creamy enough to make green grow on you!

Yield:	Prep time:	Serving size:
about 4 cups	15 minutes	2 cups

Each serving has:		
487 calories	45 g carbohydrate	26 g fat
10 g fiber	13 g protein	

½ cup hemp seeds

1 tsp. spirulina

1 TB. *matcha powder*

2 large fresh bananas, peeled

1 large pitted date

2 cups water

2 cups fresh spinach

1. In a high-speed blender, combine hemp seeds, spirulina, matcha powder, bananas, date, water, and spinach.

2. Blend until completely smooth.

Variation: Add ¼ cup lucuma powder for an earthy, maplelike flavor that complements this smoothie perfectly.

DEFINITION

Matcha powder is the product of dried and ground green tea leaves. Matcha contains a high amount of chlorophyll and packs antioxidants specific only to the tea plant. It's also a natural mood enhancer because of its theanine.

Purple Peppermint Smoothie

Creamy cashews transform this cool and minty smoothie into a delicious blueberry shake!

Yield:	Prep time:	Serving size:
about 4 cups	15 minutes	2 cups
Each serving has:		
604 calories	94 g carbohydrate	26 g fat
14 g fiber	15 g protein	

3 cups fresh or frozen blueberries	1½ cups fresh mint leaves
½ cup cashews	4 large pitted dates
	1½ cups water

1. In a high-speed blender, combine blueberries, cashews, mint leaves, dates, and water.

2. Blend until completely smooth.

Variation: For an antioxidant-rich **Chocolate Mint Smoothie,** add ¼ cup cacao.

Goji Goodness Smoothie

You'll love the simple berry flavor and smooth coconut and tapioca-like texture of this green smoothie.

Yield:	Prep time:	Serving size:
about 4 cups	15 minutes	2 cups

Each serving has:		
594 calories	115 g carbohydrate	12 g fat
17 g fiber	10 g protein	

⅓ cup goji berries

Water and meat of 1 young
    coconut

½ cup unsweetened acai

2 large pitted dates

1 cup pitted cherries

4 kale leaves, stems removed

⅛ cup chia seeds

1. In a high-speed blender, combine goji berries, coconut water and meat, acai, dates, cherries, and kale leaves.

2. Blend until completely smooth.

3. Stir in chia seeds, and let stand for 10 minutes.

Variation: If you prefer, you can use 2 cups ready-to-drink coconut milk or other milk alternative. For a richer flavor, replace the dates with 5 dried apricots.

 FRESH FACT

Goji berries are a superfood used for everything from longevity and optimum health to wilderness survival. They contain all eight essential amino acids plus tons of antioxidants. Their polysaccharides encourage the production of naturally occurring human growth hormone, which minimizes the effects of aging, and its numerous other compounds relieve the feelings of fatigue. Goji berries are a perfect combatant for the stressors of modern-day life, so enjoy!

Cherry Cream Smoothie

Cherry and almonds are a classic combination, and Incan berries enhance the slight tartness of cherries while dates sweeten the smoothie. Cherry amaretto fans will delight!

Yield:	Prep time:	Serving size:
about 4 cups	15 minutes	2 cups

Each serving has:		
589 calories	89 g carbohydrate	26 g fat
10 g fiber	14 g protein	

2½ cups pitted, fresh or frozen cherries

⅓ cup almond butter

⅓ cup Incan berries

¾ cup water

1 tsp. almond extract

3 large pitted dates

4 kale leaves, stems removed

1. In a high-speed blender, combine cherries, almond butter, Incan berries, water, almond extract, dates, and kale leaves.

2. Blend until completely smooth.

Variation: To complement the flavor in this smoothie and naturally balance the sugars, add ¼ cup mesquite meal.

Green Man Smoothie

This very sweet smoothie formulated to support the modern-day male is balanced by a savory undertone.

Yield:	Prep time:	Serving size:
about 4 cups	15 minutes, plus 1 hour soak time	2 cups

Each serving has:		
370 calories	50 g carbohydrate	17 g fat
8 g fiber	13 g protein	

½ cup pumpkin seeds

2 large fresh bananas, peeled

2 cups water

1 large pitted date

1 TB. maca powder

1 TB. ginseng powder

2 cups chopped fresh parsley

1. Soak pumpkin seeds in water for at least 1 hour. Drain and rinse.

2. In a high-speed blender, combine bananas, soaked pumpkin seeds, water, date, maca powder, ginseng powder, and parsley.

3. Blend until completely smooth.

Variation: For added protection of the male reproductive organs, add 1 tablespoon saw palmetto powder.

BLENDER BLUNDER

Pumpkin seeds are a wonderful tonic and muscle-building food, but be aware that many pumpkin seeds sold in supermarkets are rancid. Large numbers of broken seeds and a yellowish color indicate bad seeds and should be avoided. Ask your local grocer to keep a fresh supply, and keep them refrigerated or frozen to preserve shelf life.

Green Goddess Smoothie

This smoothie is formulated to tone the female body, and you won't even think of reaching for the chocolate ice cream after you try this rich, nutrient-dense delight!

Yield:	Prep time:	Serving size:
about 4 cups	15 minutes	2 cups

Each serving has:		
819 calories	110 g carbohydrate	31 g fat
24 g fiber	33 g protein	

1 cup raspberry leaf tea	⅓ cup dried figs
½ cup fresh or frozen raspberries	½ cup hemp seeds
	¼ cup raw cacao powder
2 cups fresh figs	1 TB. maca powder
¼ cup goji berries	2 cups fresh nettles

1. In a high-speed blender, combine raspberry leaf tea, raspberries, fresh figs, goji berries, figs, hemp seeds, raw cacao powder, maca powder, and nettles.

2. Blend until completely smooth.

Variation: For extra hormonal balancing, add 1 teaspoon shatavari powder. For use during pregnancy, omit the raspberry leaf tea, leave out the shatavari, and use rooibos tea as a base instead.

TO YOUR HEALTH!

Raspberry leaf tea and nettle are uterine tonics that support healthy menstruation. These two herbs are safe for use during the last trimester of pregnancy and while nursing; however, raspberry leaf is better avoided during the first two trimesters, so that's when you'd use rooibos as a base. Hemp seeds are rich in most vitamins, minerals, amino acids, and omegas. They are easily digested, making them very useful for any stage in a woman's life. Combine that with calcium-rich figs, the abundant magnesium in cacao, and all the nutrients in the goji berries, and you have a beautiful, synergistic blend of super nutrition and amazing flavor.

Super Human Smoothie

This bold smoothie sweetens the bitter taste of tonic herbs and coaxes them into delicious harmony with creamy hemp seeds.

Yield:	Prep time:	Serving size:
about 4 cups	15 minutes, plus 1 hour soak time	2 cups

Each serving has:		
621 calories	100 g carbohydrate	19 g fat
13 g fiber	24 g protein	

½ cup goji berries	1 TB. ashwagandha powder
⅓ cup hemp seeds	1 TB. reishi mushroom powder
2 large pitted dates	4 kale leaves, stems removed
1 large fresh banana, peeled	1½ cups water
2 TB. maca powder	

1. Soak goji berries in water to cover for at least 1 hour. Drain and rinse.

2. In a high-speed blender, combine hemp seeds, dates, banana, soaked goji berries, maca powder, ashwagandha powder, reishi mushroom powder, kale leaves, and 1½ cups water.

3. Blend until completely smooth.

Variation: For a more calcium-rich smoothie, replace the dates and banana in this recipe with 5 dried figs.

Smoothies for Weight Loss

In This Chapter

- Satisfying hunger with nutrition
- Feeling full and satisfied
- A fresh approach to weight loss

Green smoothies are truly the optimal weight-loss tool. Even if you change nothing else in your diet, simply adding a daily 2-cup smoothie made with leafy greens will help optimize your weight. For rapid weight loss the healthy way, green smoothies are an essential tool for any weight-management program.

The most effective weight-loss smoothies are made with very simple ingredients—only greens, whole fruits, and vegetables. They take very little energy for your body to digest, leaving ample time and resources for your body to devote to cleansing and releasing excess weight.

The high-quality nutrition and low calorie content in these smoothies is a cornerstone to easy weight maintenance. They contribute to a diminished or slightly suppressed appetite because when nutrition requirements are met, the appetite is satisfied and the feeling of constant, nagging hunger disappears. So even though a smoothie digests quickly, it keeps you feeling satisfied longer than a traditional meal.

Another huge reason green smoothies contribute to weight loss is that fibrous green leaves add bulk to smoothies and really make your stomach feel full. This sensation is often a huge contributing factor to whether or not a weight-loss program is successful. When you feel full and nourished, it's easier to avoid snacking between meals and to make healthier meal choices throughout the entire day.

Even if you're already at your ideal weight, the smoothies in this chapter are well worth trying. The simple ingredients in these recipes make them very accessible, and you won't have to go out of your way to find exotic ingredients or superfoods.

Wild Green Smoothie

This mild and refreshing smoothie is great for your everyday weight-loss program. It's not overly sweet, not at all bitter, and has just a hint of tartness.

Yield:	Prep time:	Serving size:
about 4 cups	15 minutes	2 cups

Each serving has:		
140 calories	31 g carbohydrate	1 g fat
2 g fiber	4 g protein	

2 cups chopped cucumber	⅛ cup fresh lemon juice
3 medium oranges, peeled and sectioned	2 cups fresh spinach
	1 cup fresh sorrel

1. In a high-speed blender, combine cucumber, oranges, lemon juice, spinach, and sorrel.

2. Blend until completely smooth.

Variation: This recipe also works well with fresh lime or tangerine juice instead of lemon juice.

FRESH FACT

Sorrel by its very nature alkalizes the body. Its sour flavor is very tonifying to the liver, which stimulates weight loss. Sorrel also has a far more concentrated vitamin C content than oranges. If you ever feel a cold coming on or just want a nutrition boost, drink up!

Raspberry Recharge Smoothie

Delicious, tart raspberries are sweetened with light and refreshing apple juice and become a flavorful medley when combined with cilantro.

Yield:	Prep time:	Serving size:
about 4 cups	15 minutes	2 cups

Each serving has:		
178 calories	41 g carbohydrate	2 g fat
14 g fiber	4 g protein	

3 cups fresh or frozen raspberries

1 cup fresh apple juice

1½ cups chopped cucumber

2 cups chopped fresh cilantro

1. In a high-speed blender, combine raspberries, apple juice, cucumber, and cilantro.

2. Blend until completely smooth.

Variation: If cilantro seems too herbal for your preference, try 2 cups spinach instead.

Cranberry Cooler Smoothie

Tart cranberries and fresh cucumber blend perfectly with succulent pears in this tasty smoothie.

Yield:	Prep time:	Serving size:
about 4 cups	15 minutes	2 cups
Each serving has:		
178 calories	45 g carbohydrate	1 g fat
10 g fiber	2 g protein	

¾ cup water

1 TB. maple syrup

2 medium ripe pears or apples (your choice), cored and chopped

1 cup chopped cucumber

¾ cup fresh or frozen cranberries

½ cup chopped celery

½ cup chopped fresh parsley

1. In a high-speed blender, combine water, maple syrup, pears, cucumber, cranberries, celery, and parsley, layering ingredients to ensure proper blending.

2. Blend until completely smooth.

Variation: If cranberries aren't available, you can substitute other berries like blackberries or gooseberries. Also try replacing the celery with whole peeled oranges accompanied by ½ cup chopped fennel for more of a holiday flavor.

TO YOUR HEALTH!

This delicious and detoxifying smoothie makes a great Thanksgiving cocktail or a cooling summer companion. Parsley, cucumbers, and cranberries are all well known for their tonifying effects on the kidneys, which can be very helpful if you're trying to burn off heavy holiday food. Drink this in the summer to keep your electrolytes replenished in the heat and to take advantage of your body's natural tendency to detox during the warmer weather.

Cucumber Crush Smoothie

The strong herbal taste of parsley is complemented nicely by mildly sweet cucumber and a squeeze of tart lemon.

Yield:	Prep time:	Serving size:
about 4 cups	15 minutes	2 cups

Each serving has:		
80 calories	18 g carbohydrate	1 g fat
4 g fiber	4 g protein	

4 cups chopped cucumber

2 cups chopped fresh parsley

1 TB. fresh lemon juice

1. In a high-speed blender, combine cucumber, parsley, and lemon juice.

2. Blend until completely smooth.

Variation: You may add a bit of fresh apple juice to sweeten this smoothie if you like.

Strawberry Fields Smoothie

Mild greens sneak in under the potent flavor of the sweet and tart combination of strawberries and oranges.

Yield:	Prep time:	Serving size:
about 4 cups	15 minutes	2 cups

Each serving has:		
161 calories	38 g carbohydrate	1 g fat
10 g fiber	5 g protein	

3 medium oranges, peeled and sectioned	3 cups lamb's quarters leaves or other wild greens
1½ cups fresh or frozen strawberries	½ cup chopped celery

1. In a high-speed blender, combine oranges, strawberries, lamb's quarters leaves, and celery.

2. Blend until completely smooth.

Variation: For a **Berry Burner Smoothie,** replace the oranges with 1½ grapefruits, peeled and sectioned, plus 2 pitted dates to get extra fat-burning qualities without sacrificing any of the sweetness.

 BLENDER BLUNDER

Most people pick off the silica-rich strawberry leaves before eating or blending the juicy fruits. Resist that urge! Those leaves are a perfect opportunity to get minerals that may be lacking in your diet. So go ahead and throw them in whole!

Green Grapevine Smoothie

Kale and celery juice tone down the strong sweetness of blended grapes. It's still on the sweeter side, though, and very delicious.

Yield:	Prep time:	Serving size:
about 4 cups	15 minutes	2 cups

Each serving has:		
202 calories	50 g carbohydrate	1 g fat
3 g fiber	5 g protein	

2 cups fresh celery juice	3 cups red grapes
¼ cup fresh kale juice	2 cups fresh spinach

1. In a high-speed blender, combine celery juice, kale juice, red grapes, and spinach.

2. Blend until completely smooth.

Variation: You can use a whole cucumber instead of celery and kale juice in this smoothie. Also, try adding lamb's quarters in place of the spinach.

 FRESH FACT

Red grapes are rich in the antioxidant anthocyanin, which is noted for being anti-inflammatory, among a variety of other reputed benefits. Combined with celery, which tones down the sugars in the grapes and balances the electrolytes, this smoothie is ready to protect you from all kinds of oxidative stress. It's a great source of naturally occurring resveratrol, too.

Wilder Cress Smoothie

Watercress has a mustardy taste that livens up an otherwise simple smoothie. This cooling vegetable and fruit cocktail is then warmed up with a touch of spicy ginger.

Yield:	Prep time:	Serving size:
about 4 cups	15 minutes	2 cups

Each serving has:		
148 calories	37 g carbohydrate	1 g fat
7 g fiber	3 g protein	

3 cups chopped apple (your favorite)

2 cups chopped celery

1 cup chopped cucumber

2 cups chopped fresh watercress

1 (1-in.) piece fresh peeled ginger

⅛ cup fresh lemon juice

1. In a high-speed blender, combine apple, celery, cucumber, watercress, ginger, and lemon juice.

2. Blend until completely smooth.

Variation: Arugula has a very similar flavor to watercress, so if you can't find watercress, you can use an equal amount of arugula instead.

Purely Energizing Smoothie

This is a classic sweet and tart green juice blend. It tastes like green lemonade, which makes it very kid friendly!

Yield:	Prep time:	Serving size:
about 4 cups	15 minutes	2 cups

Each serving has:		
148 calories	34 g carbohydrate	1 g fat
4 g fiber	5 g protein	

1 cup fresh apple juice   ⅛ cup fresh lemon juice
1½ cups chopped celery   6 kale leaves, stems removed
1½ cups chopped cucumber

1. In a high-speed blender, combine apple juice, celery, cucumber, lemon juice, and kale leaves.

2. Blend until completely smooth.

Variation: Try adding dandelion greens in place of the kale leaves. You can also trade out the celery for an equivalent amount of chopped fennel.

TO YOUR HEALTH!

This is a very flavorful green juice combination with the fiber intact for extra cleansing action. It's not too green-tasting and is a perfect place to start if you feel timid about the idea of drinking blended greens. This is a staple blend for everyday weight balance, and you may find yourself revisiting this recipe again and again because it's easy to make and tastes great!

Feelin' Grape! Smoothie

A little lemon and some earthy celery are the perfect thing to bring balance to this fresh, sweet, and juicy grape blend.

Yield:	Prep time:	Serving size:
about 4 cups	15 minutes	2 cups
Each serving has:		
228 calories	59 g carbohydrate	1 g fat
4 g fiber	3 g protein	

4 cups grapes

2 cups chopped celery

⅛ cup fresh lemon juice

1. In a high-speed blender, combine grapes, celery, and lemon juice.

2. Blend until completely smooth.

Variation: For more chlorophyll, you can add 2 kale leaves to this smoothie without overpowering the flavor.

Melon-Mint Julep Smoothie

This smoothie is a sweet, simple, and healthy take on the famous cocktail. The combination of aromatic mint and fresh watermelon will delight your taste buds.

Yield:	Prep time:	Serving size:
about 4 cups	15 minutes	2 cups

Each serving has:		
122 calories	29 g carbohydrate	1 g fat
4 g fiber	4 g protein	

3 cups chopped watermelon	½ cup fresh mint leaves
1 cup chopped celery	6 kale leaves, stems removed

1. In a high-speed blender, combine watermelon, celery, mint leaves, and kale leaves.

2. Blend until completely smooth.

Variation: Substitute any other type of melon for the watermelon.

FRESH FACT

Watermelon juice and mint are wonderfully cooling and are also incredibly cleansing foods. Surprisingly high in vitamin E, watermelon is very mineral rich. Don't bother removing the seeds; they're completely edible and contain 35 percent protein by weight. Just be sure to blend them well.

Ginger Zinger Smoothie

Like a blended ginger candy, sweet with a touch of heat from the ginger, this smoothie will put a zing in your step.

Yield:	Prep time:	Serving size:
about 4 cups	15 minutes	2 cups

Each serving has:		
193 calories	49 g carbohydrate	1 g fat
10 g fiber	3 g protein	

2 cups chopped pear	1 (2-in.) piece fresh peeled ginger
2 cups water or cucumber juice, celery juice, or your favorite	6 kale leaves, stems removed

1. In a high-speed blender, combine pears, water, and ginger.

2. Blend until completely smooth.

3. Add kale leaves, and blend until completely smooth.

Variation: For an even spicier **Hot 'n' Healthy Smoothie,** add ¼ cup fresh lemon juice and ⅛ teaspoon cayenne.

TO YOUR HEALTH!

Drink this warming smoothie to get your blood pumping prior to a workout or to give your immune system a boost during the cold season. Ginger dilates the capillaries and is toning to the circulatory system.

Purely Pear Smoothie

Mint is a lovely companion to wheatgrass and brings the mild herbal flavors of this smoothie together harmoniously.

Yield:	Prep time:	Serving size:
about 4 cups	15 minutes	2 cups

Each serving has:		
145 calories	37 g carbohydrate	0 g fat
9 g fiber	2 g protein	

3 cups chopped pear

1½ cups chopped celery

½ cup fresh mint leaves

⅛ cup fresh wheatgrass juice

1 cup water

1. In a high-speed blender, combine pear, celery, mint leaves, wheatgrass juice, and water.

2. Blend until completely smooth.

Variation: You may omit mint leaves in this recipe and add another leafy herb such as parsley or basil in its place.

Blueberry Buzz Smoothie

The blueberry flavor really comes through in this fresh smoothie. The apples and celery complement the blueberries while allowing them to take center stage.

Yield:	Prep time:	Serving size:
about 4 cups	15 minutes	2 cups

Each serving has:		
166 calories	43 g carbohydrate	1 g fat
7 g fiber	2 g protein	

1 cup water

1 TB. maple syrup

1 cup fresh or frozen blueberries

1 cup chopped celery

2 cups chopped apple (your favorite)

1. In a high-speed blender, combine water, maple syrup, blueberries, celery, and apple.

2. Blend until completely smooth.

Variation: This smoothie also tastes great with kale instead of celery. Or for a **Banana Blues Smoothie,** add 1 large banana and about 4 kale leaves in place of the apple.

TO YOUR HEALTH!

The blueberries in this smoothie make it very kid-friendly, and the maple syrup adds just enough sweetness to make young ones overlook how healthy it really is for them. Drink this smoothie when you feel like going easier on the greens but still want to reap their benefits.

Citrus Squeeze Smoothie

In this smoothie, the cleansing benefits of sweet yet astringent grapefruit combine with tart cranberries and are sweetened with a bit of maple syrup. Simple, cleansing, and delicious.

Yield:	Prep time:	Serving size:
about 4 cups	15 minutes	2 cups

Each serving has:		
231 calories	55 g carbohydrate	1 g fat
4 g fiber	4 g protein	

2½ cups fresh grapefruit juice
1 cup fresh or frozen cranberries

4 kale leaves, stems removed
2 TB. maple syrup

1. In a high-speed blender, combine grapefruit juice, cranberries, kale leaves, and maple syrup.

2. Blend until completely smooth.

Variation: This smoothie is also tasty with 1 cup raspberries instead of the cranberries.

Greener Grasses Smoothie

Although *wheatgrass juice* is generally very strong-tasting, it's complemented and masked very well in this smoothie, thanks to a generous amount of ginger and lemon.

Yield:	Prep time:	Serving size:
about 4 cups	15 minutes	2 cups
Each serving has:		
114 calories	28 g carbohydrate	1 g fat
3 g fiber	2 g protein	

⅛ cup fresh wheatgrass juice

1 cup chopped cucumber

1 cup fresh apple juice

2 cups chopped celery

¼ cup fresh lemon juice

2 TB. fresh ginger juice

1. In a high-speed blender, combine wheatgrass juice, cucumber, apple juice, celery, lemon juice, and ginger juice.

2. Blend until completely smooth.

Variation: You can omit the cucumber, apple juice, and celery and instead use 2 cups chopped pear and 5 kale leaves. Try adding ⅛ teaspoon cayenne for extra cleansing power.

DEFINITION

Wheatgrass juice is the liquid pressed from the blades of wheatgrass or barley grass. It's about 70 percent chlorophyll and contains all 8 essential amino acids plus 4 additional ones, making it a viable source of highly digestible protein. It can sometimes be hard to get past the taste, but when balanced with other flavors, such as in this green smoothie, it actually can be quite enjoyable.

Liquid Garden Smoothie

Parsley and lemon complement the other flavors in this sweet and savory smoothie in a way that both tones down and brings out the flavor of the other vegetables.

Yield:	Prep time:	Serving size:
about 4 cups	15 minutes	2 cups

Each serving has:		
92 calories	21 g carbohydrate	1 g fat
3 g fiber	4 g protein	

½ cup fresh beet juice

1 cup fresh carrot juice

1 cup chopped celery

1 cup chopped cucumber

¼ cup fresh lemon juice

1 cup chopped fresh cilantro

1 cup chopped fresh parsley

1. In a high-speed blender, combine beet juice, carrot juice, celery, cucumber, and lemon juice.

2. Blend until completely smooth.

3. Add cilantro and parsley, and blend until completely smooth.

Variation: For a **Garden Variety Smoothie,** replace the carrot juice with 1½ cups fresh tomatoes and add ½ cup fresh basil.

Healing Smoothies

In This Chapter

- Green smoothies, nature's healing food
- Use flavor balancing to benefit from healing foods
- Recipes for healing what ails you

Numerous fruits, vegetables, and greens are particularly healing for your digestive tract and, in fact, your entire body. Healing foods assist the body in its cleansing processes while also correcting nutritional deficiencies. They support normal production of healthy cells throughout the body, boost nonspecific immunity, and keep the body in its ideal, alkaline pH. They also support the endocrine system in its production of various hormones and relieve an overburdened pancreas by balancing blood sugar levels.

In general, green smoothies are incredibly healing and can have a variety of positive effects. If you have digestive issues, you'll find relief from the recipes in this chapter. If you have blemished skin, purify yourself from the inside out and discover your true glowing complexion. Whatever ails you, find balance in healing green smoothies by making them a central part of your daily diet.

Many of these foods tend to be bitter, astringent, sour, or pungent. If you're not a fan of such intense flavors, never fear. The wonderful and potent healing green smoothie recipes we've developed for this chapter help you discover ways to enjoy the incredible flavors of healing plant foods. Give your taste buds a treat by exploring these delicious, healing smoothies!

Green Sea Smoothie

Mild and savory *dulse* adds complexity to this zingy and fresh smoothie. This is a potent drink everyone can enjoy.

Yield:	Prep time:	Serving size:
about 4 cups	15 minutes	2 cups

Each serving has:		
235 calories	14 g carbohydrate	21 g fat
3 g fiber	2 g protein	

3 TB. flaxseed oil

⅛ cup fresh wheatgrass juice

2½ cups chopped cucumber

2 cups chopped celery

⅓ cup fresh lemon juice

⅛ cup whole dulse or dulse flakes

1 cup water

1. In a high-speed blender, combine flaxseed oil, wheatgrass juice, cucumber, celery, lemon juice, dulse, and water.

2. Blend until completely smooth.

Variation: For a milder-tasting smoothie, replace the wheatgrass juice with 5 kale leaves, stems removed.

DEFINITION

Dulse is a savory sea vegetable used as a source of protein and the trace minerals necessary to the human body. It's generally thought of as being a seaweed, but in fact, *palmaria palmata* is a purple-colored red algae.

Cleansing Cranberry Smoothie

This tart smoothie leaves you with a sweet aftertaste. Cleansing cranberry and cucumber make a clean, fresh combination with the complementary flavor of sorrel.

Yield:	Prep time:	Serving size:
about 4 cups	15 minutes	2 cups

Each serving has:		
155 calories	26 g carbohydrate	5 g fat
12 g fiber	5 g protein	

3 cups chopped cucumber

2 cups fresh or frozen cranberries

2 TB. chia seeds

3 cups fresh sorrel

1 cup water

1. In a high-speed blender, combine cucumber, cranberries, chia seeds, sorrel, and water.

2. Blend until completely smooth.

Variation: For a slightly sweet **Cleansing Cranberry Orange Smoothie,** replace the water with 1 cup orange juice.

Cleanse Master Smoothie

This smoothie is very well balanced in the flavor department. Sour, sweet, salty, bitter, spicy—it's all here.

Yield:	Prep time:	Serving size:
about 4 cups	15 minutes	2 cups

Each serving has:		
334 calories	39 g carbohydrate	22 g fat
9 g fiber	5 g protein	

2 medium whole lemons, peeled

2 cups chopped apple (your favorite)

1 cup chopped celery

3 TB. flaxseed oil

6 kale leaves, stems removed

½ tsp. cayenne

½ tsp. sea salt

⅔ cup water

1. In a high-speed blender, combine lemons, apple, celery, flaxseed oil, kale leaves, cayenne, sea salt, and water.

2. Blend until completely smooth.

Variation: For a **Clean Earth Smoothie,** add a 1-inch piece each fresh peeled ginger and turmeric root.

TO YOUR HEALTH!

This fiber-filled smoothie is a well-balanced take on the popular cleansing drink made with fresh lemon juice, cayenne, and maple syrup. My version supplies the fiber necessary for cleansing, as well as the extra benefit of liver-tonifying flaxseed oil. Make this smoothie a part of your daily morning health program.

Pure Melon Smoothie

Sweet, juicy watermelon blends perfectly with sour lime, while the cinnamon gives this blend some warmth, and fresh kale brings all the flavors together.

Yield:	Prep time:	Serving size:
about 4 cups	15 minutes	2 cups

Each serving has:		
159 calories	39 g carbohydrate	1 g fat
3 g fiber	5 g protein	

5 cups chopped watermelon	1 TB. ground cinnamon
⅓ cup fresh lime juice	6 kale leaves, stems removed

1. In a high-speed blender, combine watermelon, lime juice, ground cinnamon, and kale leaves.

2. Blend until completely smooth.

Variation: Try using another green in this recipe, such as spinach.

Digestive De-Stressor Smoothie

Mild-tasting and very slightly sweet, this smoothie has what you need to ditch your digestive issues.

Yield:	Prep time:	Serving size:
about 4 cups	15 minutes	2 cups
Each serving has:		
57 calories	13 g carbohydrate	0 g fat
4 g fiber	3 g protein	

3 cups chopped cabbage

3 cups chopped cucumber

1 (2-in.) piece fresh peeled turmeric

1¼ cups water

1. In a high-speed blender, combine cabbage, cucumber, turmeric, and water.

2. Blend until completely smooth.

Variation: Try adding ⅛ teaspoon cayenne for some heat. You may also add ⅛ cup fresh wheatgrass juice if you prefer some extra green cleansing power.

TO YOUR HEALTH!

This smoothie has very pure ingredients that support digestive health. Cabbage is sometimes known as "rich food for the poor man." It's very easy to acquire and is reasonably priced, yet it's one of the most powerful healing and nutrifying foods on the planet. If you suffer from metabolic diseases or chronic digestive disorders, drink this smoothie often. You may also use this smoothie topically for acne or dull skin.

Amazing Enzyme Smoothie

Sweet pineapple has a nice acid flavor that balances with the intensity of wheatgrass.

Yield:	Prep time:	Serving size:
about 4 cups	15 minutes	2 cups

Each serving has:		
144 calories	36 g carbohydrate	0 g fat
5 g fiber	2 g protein	

3 cups chopped pineapple	⅛ cup fresh wheatgrass juice
2 cups chopped celery	1 cup water

1. In a high-speed blender, combine pineapple, celery, wheatgrass juice, and water.

2. Blend until completely smooth.

Variation: For a **Tart 'n' Tangy Smoothie,** add ¼ cup fresh lemon juice and ⅛ teaspoon cayenne.

Sweet Grass Smoothie

Earthy celery balances the sweetness of grapes and wheatgrass, while aloe gives this smoothie a creamy texture.

Yield:	Prep time:	Serving size:
about 4 cups	15 minutes	2 cups
Each serving has:		
230 calories	59 g carbohydrate	1 g fat
4 g fiber	3 g protein	

4 cups grapes

½ cup filleted aloe vera

⅛ cup fresh wheatgrass juice

2 cups chopped celery

1. In a high-speed blender, combine grapes, aloe vera, wheatgrass juice, and celery.

2. Blend until completely smooth.

Variation: For another version of this smoothie, replace the grapes with 3 cups chopped pear or swap out the celery with 2 cups chopped cucumber.

TO YOUR HEALTH!

Grapes, aloe vera, and wheatgrass are a trifecta of healing foods. Antiseptic grapes contain phytochemicals that are powerful solvents of inorganic residues that build up in the body. Aloe is packed with organic acids, phytonutrients, vitamins, and trace minerals. Wheatgrass has a medicinal amount of detoxifying and healing chlorophyll. Together, they soothe the entire digestive system and cleanse the body.

Dandy Detoxifier Smoothie

Apple-sweetened grapefruit and ginger mellow the dandelion greens in this wonderfully warming and cleansing smoothie.

Yield:	Prep time:	Serving size:
about 4 cups	15 minutes	2 cups

Each serving has:		
182 calories	45 g carbohydrate	1 g fat
7 g fiber	3 g protein	

3 cups chopped apple (your favorite)

1 cup chopped cucumber

1 (2-in.) piece fresh peeled ginger

2 cups chopped dandelion greens

1 cup fresh grapefruit juice

1. In a high-speed blender, combine apple, cucumber, ginger, dandelion greens, and grapefruit juice.

2. Blend until completely smooth.

Variation: For a more intense, nutrient-dense smoothie, omit the grapefruit juice and add 1 teaspoon spirulina instead.

Cactus Cleanser Smoothie

This simple, slightly sweet smoothie is very light on the palate with a hint of creaminess.

Yield:	Prep time:	Serving size:
about 4 cups	15 minutes	2 cups

Each serving has:		
150 calories	24 g carbohydrate	5 g fat
10 g fiber	6 g protein	

3 cups chopped pear	2 TB. chia seeds
1 cup filleted *nopal cactus,* chopped	6 kale leaves, stems removed
	2 cups water

1. In a high-speed blender, combine pear, nopal cactus, chia seeds, kale leaves, and water.

2. Blend until completely smooth.

Variation: If you can't find fresh nopal cactus leaves, substitute fresh leaf with 3 powdered nopal cactus capsules or 1 cup filleted aloe vera.

DEFINITION

Nopal cactus, also known as *nopales,* is a cactus commonly eaten in Mexico. It's proven to benefit diabetics by buffering sugar absorption, making it helpful for balancing blood sugar for those with chronic issues. Nopal cactus leaves are also known as prickly pear cactus and can be found in many health food stores and international markets.

Lemon Burst Smoothie

This very warming, sweet, sour, and spicy smoothie spares nothing in flavor or rejuvenating power.

Yield:	Prep time:	Serving size:
about 4 cups	15 minutes	2 cups

Each serving has:		
168 calories	43 g carbohydrate	1 g fat
8 g fiber	4 g protein	

½ cup fresh lemon juice

2 cups chopped cabbage

3 cups chopped apple (your favorite)

1 (3-in.) piece fresh peeled ginger

½ tsp. cayenne

3 kale leaves, stems removed

½ cup water

1. In a high-speed blender, combine lemon juice, cabbage, apple, ginger, cayenne, kale leaves, and water.

2. Blend until completely smooth.

Variation: This smoothie packs a flavor punch, but if you want to take it to the next level and make a **Not-So-Mellow Yellow Smoothie,** replace the water with 1 cup grapefruit juice and add 1 (2-inch) piece fresh peeled turmeric.

Ginger Gem Smoothie

Perfectly sweet watermelon and slightly astringent, sour cranberries blend warming ginger and cooling aloe into a very well-balanced smoothie tonic for any season.

Yield:	Prep time:	Serving size:
about 4 cups	15 minutes	2 cups
Each serving has:		
170 calories	40 g carbohydrate	1 g fat
6 g fiber	6 g protein	

1 cup fresh or frozen cranberries

4 cups chopped watermelon

½ cup filleted aloe vera

1 (3-in.) piece fresh peeled ginger

6 kale leaves, stems removed

1. In a high-speed blender, combine cranberries, watermelon, aloe vera, ginger, and kale leaves.

2. Blend until completely smooth.

Variation: If fresh red or black currents grow in your area, omit cranberries in this recipe and add the same amount of fresh currents for some local nutrition.

Blood Builder Smoothie

Ripe pears round out the sharp flavor of collards and bitter burdock in this earthy and sweet smoothie that will give your circulatory system a boost of oxygen.

Yield:	Prep time:	Serving size:
about 4 cups	15 minutes	2 cups

Each serving has:		
156 calories	40 g carbohydrate	1 g fat
10 g fiber	3 g protein	

3 cups chopped pear

1 cup chopped celery

1 (5-in.) piece fresh unpeeled burdock, brushed clean

1 (2-in.) piece fresh peeled turmeric

6 collard greens, stems removed

1 cup water

1. In a high-speed blender, combine pear, celery, burdock, turmeric, collard greens, and water.

2. Blend until completely smooth.

Variation: Try adding ¼ cup fresh lemon juice and ⅛ teaspoon cayenne to this smoothie for an added kick.

TO YOUR HEALTH!

Burdock is a liver and blood purifier. It's been noted as being potentially helpful for a wide range of disorders, including psoriasis, hepatitis, tumors, arthritis, certain types of heavy metal poisoning, and several types of cancer. It isn't necessary to have a chronic disorder to reap the benefits of burdock, so use it regularly to give your hard-working liver some extra support.

Ginger Berry Smoothie

Like a blended ginger candy, sweet with a touch of heat from the ginger, this smoothie will put a spring in your step.

Yield:	Prep time:	Serving size:
about 4 cups	15 minutes	2 cups

Each serving has:		
208 calories	49 g carbohydrate	2 g fat
16 g fiber	7 g protein	

3 cups fresh or frozen blackberries	1 (2-in.) piece fresh, peeled ginger
2 cups chopped apple (your favorite)	6 kale leaves, stems removed
	½ cup water

1. In a high-speed blender, combine blackberries, apple, ginger, kale leaves, and water.

2. Blend until completely smooth.

Variation: Many wonderful varieties of berries are often overlooked in commercial markets. Replace blackberries in this recipe with any of these local berries, such as loganberry, marionberry, gooseberry, mulberry, or salmon berry.

Mint Cooler Smoothie

Sweet ripe pears and crisp celery create the perfect base for the tingling mint that will refresh your entire being.

Yield:	Prep time:	Serving size:
about 4 cups	15 minutes	2 cups
Each serving has:		
171 calories	43 g carbohydrate	1 g fat
12 g fiber	3 g protein	

3 cups chopped pear

3 cups chopped celery

2 cups fresh mint leaves

1 cup water

1. In a high-speed blender, combine pear, celery, mint leaves, and water.

2. Blend until completely smooth.

Variation: Use any of the popular mint varieties you like in this smoothie. You'll get a different flavor from the piercing zing of spearmint, the fresh cooling sensation of common mint, or the deep flavor of chocolate mint. This smoothie is also wonderful with 1 (2-inch) piece fresh ginger.

Inner Rejuvenator Smoothie

The deep, earthy sweetness of fresh carrot juice stirs up spicy daikon and pure cucumber into the perfect digestive rejuvenating smoothie.

Yield:	Prep time:	Serving size:
about 4 cups	15 minutes	2 cups

Each serving has:		
107 calories	24 g carbohydrate	1 g fat
4 g fiber	4 g protein	

2 cups fresh carrot juice	2 cups chopped cucumber
½ cup chopped daikon radish	2 cups chopped dandelion greens

1. In a high-speed blender, combine carrot juice, daikon radish, cucumber, and dandelion greens.

2. Blend until completely smooth.

Variation: You may swap out the daikon radish with any other type of radish based on availability and preference. For added variation, replace 1½ cups carrot juice with 1½ cups fresh beet juice.

BLENDER BLUNDER

Not all radishes are created equal! Daikon is a watery radish that's pungent but mellow compared to red or black radishes. Play it on the safe side and use daikon radishes in this recipe.

Golden Grass Smoothie

The golden glow of turmeric imparts its warm, mild, mustardlike taste to the sweet taste of wheatgrass. Water-rich celery balances these flavors with dandelion for a pleasant and refreshing smoothie.

Yield:	Prep time:	Serving size:
about 4 cups	15 minutes	2 cups

Each serving has:		
68 calories	14 g carbohydrate	1 g fat
5 g fiber	3 g protein	

¼ cup fresh wheatgrass juice

1 (3-in.) piece fresh peeled turmeric

2 cups chopped celery

2 cups chopped cucumber

2 cups chopped dandelion greens

1½ cups water

1. In a high-speed blender, combine wheatgrass juice, turmeric, celery, cucumber, dandelion greens, and water.

2. Blend until completely smooth.

Variation: For an **Eat the Weeds Smoothie,** add 1 (2-inch) piece fresh peeled ginger and 1 cup chopped apple (your favorite) to tone down the flavor of wheatgrass.

Green Smoothie Tonics

In This Chapter

- What is a tonic?
- Medicinal herbs with magical properties
- Green smoothie recipes with a tonic effect

A tonic is a substance with medicinal qualities. In this chapter, the word *tonic* refers to the toning, purifying, cleansing, and healing effects numerous herbs, spices, fruits, vegetables, and greens have on the human body. These plants are packed with phytonutrient activity that repairs soft tissues on a cellular level. Green smoothies make an ideal base for many tonic ingredients that have somewhat stronger flavors.

Many of the tonic ingredients found in these recipes may sound exotic but are very easy to find in any natural foods store that carries herbs in their supplement section. On some occasions, you may need to open a few capsules of packaged herbs if you're unable to find them in bulk. Then again, you may also want to just take encapsulated herbs along with your smoothie if you find any of them bitter. You'll still be reaping the benefits of an ultra-healing, tonic green smoothie.

The smoothies in this chapter are somewhat similar to healing smoothies but they have the added benefit of delivering particularly potent ingredients. The flavors of these smoothies are more complex than those found in other chapters. Some are sweet, some are savory, and some do taste a bit medicinal.

Jamu Spice Smoothie

This exotic health drink brings the flavors of a foreign land to your palate. Pungent, sweet, and herbaceous, this green smoothie will have your taste buds buzzing.

Yield:	Prep time:	Serving size:
about 4 cups	15 minutes, plus 2 hours soak time	2 cups

Each serving has:		
259 calories	64 g carbohydrate	2 g fat
7 g fiber	6 g protein	

⅓ cup raisins

½ cup raisin soak water

1 (5-in.) piece fresh peeled turmeric

1 tsp. ashwagandha powder

1 (1-in.) piece fresh peeled ginger

⅛ cup fresh lemon juice

⅛ tsp. ground cloves

½ cup chopped fresh fennel

6 kale leaves, stems removed

2 cups water

1. Soak raisins in water to cover for 2 hours or until they expand to ½ cup.

2. In a high-speed blender, combine soaked raisins, raisin soak water, turmeric, ashwagandha powder, ginger, lemon juice, ground cloves, fennel, kale leaves, and water.

3. Blend until completely smooth.

Variation: You may find it easier to use 1 tablespoon powdered turmeric in place of fresh turmeric. Also substitute 1 teaspoon fennel seeds if fresh fennel isn't available. This drink will also taste wonderful with soaked prunes in the place of soaked raisins. Play around and find your favorite variation!

FRESH FACT

In Bali and Java, jamu is a popular drink made from medicinal herbs, fruits, and barks, among other ingredients. These drinks are consumed for nearly every ailment and contain many different ingredients. While there are hundreds of different preparations for jamu, I've included some of the more common, widely available ingredients for this herbal green smoothie.

Pine Purifier Smoothie

Pine nuts smooth out this basil-loaded smoothie that has just a touch of tartness and an incredibly grounding effect on the mind.

Yield:	Prep time:	Serving size:
about 4 cups	15 minutes	2 cups

Each serving has:		
221 calories	16 g carbohydrate	18 g fat
5 g fiber	6 g protein	

¼ cup pine nuts

1 cup chopped tomato

2½ cups chopped cucumber

⅛ cup fresh lemon juice

2 cups fresh basil leaves

1½ cups water

1. In a high-speed blender, combine pine nuts, tomato, cucumber, lemon juice, basil leaves, and water.

2. Blend until completely smooth.

Variation: Basil is the main flavor in this smoothie, and if you want even more pure basil flavor, try replacing tomatoes with 1 cup chopped celery and omit the lemon juice.

Chai Charge Smoothie

Wonderfully warming and comforting chai spices make this deeply nourishing and purifying smoothie a sweet and creamy spiced tonic for balancing digestive health.

Yield:	Prep time:	Serving size:
about 4 cups	15 minutes	2 cups

Each serving has:		
273 calories	37 g carbohydrate	14 g fat
11 g fiber	7 g protein	

¼ cup raw tahini	½ tsp. ground cardamom
2 cups chopped pear	1 TB. ground cinnamon
4 dried figs	⅛ tsp. ground black pepper
1 (1-in.) piece fresh peeled ginger	1½ cups chopped dandelion greens
1 tsp. ground cloves	2 cups water

1. In a high-speed blender, combine tahini, pear, figs, ginger, ground cloves, ground cardamom, ground cinnamon, ground black pepper, dandelion greens, and water.

2. Blend until completely smooth.

Variation: For a sweeter smoothie, replace figs with 4 large pitted dates, and use 1½ cups fresh spinach in place of the dandelion greens.

 TO YOUR HEALTH!

This smoothie is a calcium powerhouse. Figs and sesame seeds are two of the richest plant sources for food-based calcium and many other essential minerals. The spices in this smoothie are used throughout the world to ease a variety of digestive issues and maintain healthy circulation. They're also the base of chai tea.

Italian Tonic Smoothie

The savory herbs in this smoothie blend nicely with the mild heat in zingy arugula. Tomato, celery, and lemon create a mild base that supports the more complex flavors in this harmonious medley.

Yield:	Prep time:	Serving size:
about 4 cups	15 minutes	2 cups

Each serving has:		
154 calories	8 g carbohydrate	14 g fat
2 g fiber	2 g protein	

2 TB. flaxseed oil	¼ cup fresh oregano leaves
½ cup chopped tomato	1 TB. fresh rosemary leaves
2 cups chopped celery	1 TB. fresh thyme leaves
¼ cup fresh lemon juice	1 cup arugula
1 tsp. ground black pepper	2 cups water

1. In a high-speed blender, combine flaxseed oil, tomato, celery, lemon juice, ground black pepper, oregano leaves, rosemary leaves, thyme leaves, arugula, and water.

2. Blend until completely smooth.

Variation: Use olive oil in place of the flaxseed oil for a more authentic Italian flavor experience.

Sweet Heat Smoothie

Mustard greens have a wasabi-like spiciness that brings life to a simple blend of sweet wheatgrass and apple, and enhances the lemon's zestiness.

Yield:	Prep time:	Serving size:
about 4 cups	15 minutes	2 cups

Each serving has:		
88 calories	22 g carbohydrate	0 g fat
5 g fiber	2 g protein	

⅛ cup wheatgrass juice

1 cup chopped celery

2 cups chopped apple (your favorite)

⅛ cup fresh lemon juice

1 cup chopped mustard greens

1½ cups water

1. In a high-speed blender, combine wheatgrass juice, celery, apple, lemon juice, mustard greens, and water.

2. Blend until completely smooth.

Variation: You can omit the apple and water and instead use 2 cups fresh apple or pear juice.

BLENDER BLUNDER

Mustard greens are very spicy. Their heat is similar to that of horseradish or wasabi. If you're wary of too much spice, go easy on the mustard greens at first. You can always add more if you like!

Southern Soother Smoothie

The clean flavors of the South come together to form this special blend. Herbaceous thyme, mild collards, and spicy cayenne blend into a sweet treat with refreshing watermelon.

Yield:	Prep time:	Serving size:
about 4 cups	15 minutes	2 cups

Each serving has:		
130 calories	32 g carbohydrate	1 g fat
3 g fiber	4 g protein	

5 cups cubed watermelon	2 TB. fresh thyme leaves
⅛ tsp. cayenne	4 collard leaves, stems removed

1. In a high-speed blender, combine watermelon, cayenne, thyme leaves, and collard leaves.

2. Blend until completely smooth.

Variation: Try adding 1 teaspoon black pepper to this smoothie for an interesting flavor variation that's also balanced according to East Indian tradition.

Deep Detox Smoothie

Cilantro's slightly floral flavor is reminiscent of a squeeze of citrus and adds character to the simple flavors of cucumber and apple. Cayenne adds extra cleansing power.

Yield:	Prep time:	Serving size:
about 4 cups	15 minutes	2 cups

Each serving has:		
97 calories	24 g carbohydrate	1 g fat
5 g fiber	2 g protein	

2 cups chopped cucumber

2 cups chopped apple (your favorite)

2 cups chopped fresh cilantro

1 tsp. chlorella

½ tsp. cayenne

1 cup water

1. In a high-speed blender, combine cucumber, apple, cilantro, chlorella, cayenne, and water.

2. Blend until completely smooth.

Variation: This smoothie is wonderful on its own, but you may substitute chlorella with an equal amount of AFA blue-green algae, spirulina, or ⅛ cup fresh wheatgrass juice.

FRESH FACT

Cilantro is a heavy metal chelator, meaning it removes heavy metals like mercury and lead from our cells and flushes them into the bloodstream. This makes it particularly important to consume cilantro with other foods that ensure proper elimination and prevent these toxins from being reabsorbed. Chlorella is a perfect companion to cilantro because it binds heavy metals, making them inert, and fibrous apples and cucumber help flush them out for good!

Immunity-Building Smoothie

This super vitamin C smoothie is a sweet and tart delight. Sour camu camu berry and sorrel are the ideal accompaniments to the pleasant sweetness and slight astringency of grapefruit.

Yield:	Prep time:	Serving size:
about 4 cups	15 minutes	2 cups

Each serving has:		
420 calories	35 g carbohydrate	1 g fat
4 g fiber	3 g protein	

3 cups fresh grapefruit juice

1 TB. camu camu powder

2 tsp. echinacea powder

3 cups fresh sorrel

1. In a high-speed blender, combine grapefruit juice, camu camu powder, echinacea powder, and sorrel.

2. Blend until completely smooth.

Variation: To maintain an ideal flavor, this smoothie is light on the tonic ingredients. But if you'd like to pump up the amount of echinacea or camu camu, feel free to add as much as you like along with 2 pitted dates to maintain the flavor.

Jing Shen Smoothie

The bitter herbs in this smoothie blend well into creamy, calcium-rich sesame and the sweet potency of goji berries and figs.

Yield:	Prep time:	Serving size:
about 4 cups	15 minutes, plus 1 hour soak time	2 cups

Each serving has:		
563 calories	71 g carbohydrate	25 g fat
15 g fiber	12 g protein	

½ cup goji berries
⅓ cup black sesame seeds
5 dried mission figs
1 TB. pine pollen
1 TB. reishi mushroom powder

2 tsp. shatavari powder (asparagus root)
1 tsp. ginseng powder
1 cup fresh nettles
2½ cups water

1. Soak goji berries in water to cover for at least 1 hour. Drain and rinse.

2. In a high-speed blender, combine black sesame seeds, mission figs, soaked goji berries, pine pollen, reishi mushroom powder, shatavari powder, ginseng powder, nettles, and water.

3. Blend until completely smooth.

Variation: Black sesame seeds are particularly indicated in this recipe, but you may omit them and add ½ cup soaked walnuts instead. You can also swap out the nettles with 2 cups fresh spinach.

TO YOUR HEALTH!

In traditional Chinese medicine, there are three basic concepts of different types of energy that preserve life in the body. These are the familiar *chi* (*qi*) and the less-familiar *jing* and *shen*. These three aspects can be compared to a burning candle, where *jing* is the candle, *chi* is the flame, and *shen* is the light from the fire. *Jing* is also said to be the material aspect of the body, whereas *chi* is the vital life force and *shen* is consciousness. Green smoothies naturally support the *chi* in the body, and in this smoothie I've added herbs to enliven *shen* and replenish *jing* for a Chinese medicine–inspired total body tonic.

Royal Rooibos Smoothie

Rooibos (redbush) tea has an earthy, nutty flavor similar to mild vanilla. It pairs wonderfully with sweet dates and wheatgrass because it subdues the intensity and brings out the sweetness of these ingredients. The chia seeds give this light smoothie some extra body and texture.

Yield:	Prep time:	Serving size:
about 4 cups	30 minutes	2 cups

Each serving has:		
349 calories	66 g carbohydrate	9 g fat
17 g fiber	8 g protein	

2 cups rooibos (redbush) tea	3 kale leaves, stems removed
⅛ cup fresh wheatgrass juice	¼ cup chia seeds
1 cup chopped celery	
5 large pitted dates	

1. In a high-speed blender, combine rooibos tea, wheatgrass juice, celery, dates, and kale leaves.

2. Blend until completely smooth.

3. Combine chia seeds with blended smoothie, and stir by hand.

4. Let stand for 10 to 15 minutes for chia seeds to gel.

Variation: For a milder-tasting smoothie, replace the wheatgrass juice with 2 more kale leaves, stems removed.

DEFINITION

Rooibos is an African plant that offers a balanced spectrum of electrolytes and antioxidants. It's commonly used in Africa to soothe nausea and is also recommended for altitude sickness.

Total Tonic Smoothie

This fresh-tasting smoothie is the perfect light meal. It has the nutrients your body needs with a mild sweet, flavor reminiscent of ginger lemonade.

Yield:	Prep time:	Serving size:
about 4 cups	15 minutes	2 cups

Each serving has:		
57 calories	14 g carbohydrate	0 g fat
3 g fiber	2 g protein	

2½ cups chopped cucumber

½ cup filleted aloe vera

¼ cup fresh wheatgrass juice

⅓ cup fresh lemon juice

1 cup chopped cabbage

1 (2-in.) piece fresh peeled ginger

1½ cups water

1. In a high-speed blender, combine cucumber, aloe vera, wheatgrass juice, lemon juice, cabbage, ginger, and water.

2. Blend until completely smooth.

Variation: Replace the wheatgrass juice in this recipe with 2 kale leaves, stems removed, or swap out the cabbage with broccoli.

Cruciferous Cleanser Smoothie

Bold broccoli is mellowed with clean cucumber juice and the zing of lemon. Fresh turmeric gives this smoothie a mild peppery or gingery taste.

Yield:	Prep time:	Serving size:
about 4 cups	15 minutes	2 cups

Each serving has:		
147 calories	37 g carbohydrate	1 g fat
8 g fiber	4 g protein	

2 cups chopped pear

2 cups chopped broccoli

1 cup fresh cucumber juice

2 cups chopped celery

⅓ cup fresh lemon juice

1 (2-in.) piece fresh peeled turmeric

1 cup water

1. In a high-speed blender, combine pear, broccoli, cucumber juice, celery, lemon juice, turmeric, and water.

2. Blend until completely smooth.

Variation: For a **Beautiful Brassica Smoothie,** swap out the broccoli for 2 cups chopped cauliflower, and add 3 kale leaves, stems removed, as well.

FRESH FACT

Cruciferous vegetables include broccoli, cauliflower, kale, cabbage, and several others. In general, cruciferous vegetables are known to be antioxidant rich and support your overall health. Studies have shown they reduce the risk of cancers that affect the breast, uterine lining, cervix, prostate, lung, colon, and liver. In fact, cruciferous vegetables are being studied for their halting effects on the growth of tumors for indicated cancers. Just another great reason to drink your broccoli!

Roots 'N' Fruits Smoothie

This sweet and earthy herbal smoothie has a bit of spice to it and is designed to stimulate your taste buds while soothing your body. It's a great choice for the cold season.

Yield:	Prep time:	Serving size:
about 4 cups	15 minutes	2 cups

Each serving has:		
173 calories	44 g carbohydrate	1 g fat
6 g fiber	3 g protein	

2 cups chopped apple (your favorite)

1 cup grapes

1 (3-in.) piece cleaned fresh burdock root

1 (1-in.) piece fresh peeled ginger

1 (2-in.) piece fresh peeled turmeric

¼ cup diced daikon radish

⅓ cup fresh lemon juice

4 kale leaves, stems removed

1 cup water

1. In a high-speed blender, combine apple, grapes, burdock root, ginger, turmeric, daikon radish, lemon juice, kale leaves, and water.

2. Blend until completely smooth.

Variation: For an extra kick, add 2 tablespoons fresh minced horseradish.

Chyawanyaprash Tea Smoothie

This herbal tonic smoothie has flavors reminiscent of chai, but it's also very tart.

Yield:	Prep time:	Serving size:
about 4 cups	15 minutes	2 cups

Each serving has:		
552 calories	145 g carbohydrate	1 g fat
10 g fiber	7 g protein	

⅔ cup raisins

2 cups chopped celery

1 (2-in.) piece fresh peeled turmeric

1 (1-in.) piece fresh peeled ginger

1 TB. amla berry powder

1 TB. shatavari powder

2 tsp. fenugreek powder

1 TB. ground cinnamon

1 tsp. ground cardamom

⅛ tsp. cayenne

⅛ cup fresh lemon juice

2 kale leaves, stems removed

1½ cups water (including raisin soak water)

1. Soak raisins in water to cover for a minimum of 1 hour. Drain, retaining soak water, and rinse raisins.

2. In a high-speed blender, combine soaked raisins, celery, turmeric, ginger, amla berry powder, shatavari powder, fenugreek powder, ground cinnamon, ground cardamom, cayenne, lemon juice, kale leaves, and water.

3. Blend until completely smooth.

Variation: For a smoother-textured smoothie, soak the ground spices in 2 cups boiling water for 20 minutes and strain.

FRESH FACT

Chyawanyaprash is an ancient Ayurvedic preparation of various herbs traditionally combined with honey or sugar and ghee. It's a highly bioactive, antioxidant tonic used as a folk remedy for correcting and preventing the digestive issues that lead to other diseases. It's reputed as being a longevity tonic that restores youthfulness and vigor to those who drink it regularly.

Rise 'N' Shine! Smoothie

This tonic smoothie is the perfect solution for those who aren't "morning people." The extra-spicy kick revs up your circulatory system, and the chocolate provides a nice alternative to coffee. It's light on your digestive system and packed with nutrition.

Yield:	Prep time:	Serving size:
about 4 cups	15 minutes	2 cups

Each serving has:		
409 calories	63 g carbohydrate	13 g fat
28 g fiber	15 g protein	

8 dried figs	1 TB. ginseng powder
¼ cup chia seeds	1 tsp. cayenne
1 TB. ground cinnamon	3 cups water
⅓ cup raw cacao powder	

1. In a high-speed blender, combine figs, chia seeds, ground cinnamon, raw cacao powder, ginseng powder, cayenne, and water.

2. Blend until completely smooth.

Variation: Fresh figs are preferable to dried but have a short season. When fresh figs are in season, use 6 fresh figs in place of the dried ones, and omit 1 cup water.

Smoothies for Athletes

In This Chapter

- Nutrients for bodies in motion
- Fuel without fullness
- Smoothies designed for any athlete

A 400-pound gorilla eats a diet comprised of about 84 percent fruits, leaves, bark, stems, and shoots. The other percentage is made up mostly of nuts, seeds, and insects. If an animal built of such an immense amount of lean muscle can survive and thrive on a plant-based diet, then any normally functioning human can do the same. Green smoothies give you radiant skin, mineral-dense bones, and strong and lean muscles to keep you active and full of energy throughout any stage of life.

It takes more than just protein to fuel an energetic and powerful body; it takes the nutrition of real, whole-plant foods. Protein is just one inseparable part of a whole system of nutrients needed to energize and sustain an active body. Regardless of whether you're a walker, runner, yogi, or professional athlete, you can easily acquire stamina-supporting calories, electrolytes, and potent, energizing phytonutrients from super-powered green smoothies.

Many people choose to fuel up before working out rather than burn calories on an empty stomach. However, it can be uncomfortable to hit the gym or go for a run on a full stomach. Green smoothies keep you moving without making you feel overly full or lethargic the way many traditional, difficult-to-digest protein shakes and bars will. All the same, it's best to drink any smoothie at least 1 hour before your workout so you have access to the nourishment it offers during your workout.

Go for high quality, and give your body the clean-burning calories and dense nutrition of a green smoothie so you can perform at your best every time!

Maca Mover Smoothie

This purely indulgent sweet smoothie has a rich texture similar to fresh, creamy tapioca. The smoothie base is thinner than many of the others in this chapter, but it's bulked up with the notorious 24-hour energy seed, chia!

Yield:	Prep time:	Serving size:
about 4 cups	30 minutes	2 cups

Each serving has:		
1,070 calories	105 g carbohydrate	70 g fat
29 g fiber	23 g protein	

2½ cups Brazil nut milk	5 large pitted dates
¼ cup coconut butter	6 kale leaves, stems removed
⅛ cup maca powder	¼ cup chia seeds
¼ cup lucuma powder	

1. In a high-speed blender, combine Brazil nut milk, coconut butter, maca powder, lucuma powder, dates, and kale leaves.

2. Blend until completely smooth.

3. Combine chia seeds with blended smoothie, and stir by hand.

4. Let stand for 10 to 15 minutes for chia seeds to gel.

Variation: Use your favorite nut milk in place of the Brazil nut milk, and add 2 tablespoons Brazil nut protein or other protein powder.

FRESH FACT

Brazil nuts are a rich source of protein and trace minerals. They also happen to make an incredible-tasting nut milk! Likewise, maca delivers a considerably large amount of calories in the form of protein. This luscious green smoothie packs a whopping 23 grams protein per serving without using any protein supplements!

Perfect Protein Smoothie

Sweet bananas and cashews give a wonderful thickness to this smoothie that's a cornucopia of trace minerals and electrolytes.

Yield:	Prep time:	Serving size:
about 4 cups	15 minutes	2 cups

Each serving has:		
479 calories	65 g carbohydrate	20 g fat
9 g fiber	21 g protein	

⅓ cup cashews

3 medium fresh bananas, peeled

⅛ cup sprouted brown rice protein powder

2 cups chopped celery

1 TB. spirulina

3 cups water

1. In a high-speed blender, combine cashews, bananas, sprouted brown rice protein powder, celery, spirulina, and water.

2. Blend until completely smooth.

Variation: Make a simplified version of this smoothie by replacing the celery and spirulina with 5 kale leaves, stems removed.

Beaucoup Berries Smoothie

Creamy, chocolaty, and just a touch tart, this smoothie has big berry flavor with almond undertones.

Yield:	Prep time:	Serving size:
about 4 cups	15 minutes	2 cups

Each serving has:		
527 calories	62 g carbohydrate	22 g fat
19 g fiber	26 g protein	

1½ cups fresh or frozen raspberries	⅛ cup sprouted brown rice protein powder
¼ cup goji berries	2 cups fresh spinach
¼ cup raw cacao powder	2 cups water
¼ cup almond butter	

1. In a high-speed blender, combine raspberries, goji berries, raw cacao powder, almond butter, sprouted brown rice protein powder, spinach, and water.

2. Blend until completely smooth.

Variation: You could replace the raw cacao powder with 2 tablespoons fresh lemon juice to enhance the berry flavor.

BLENDER BLUNDER

Sprouted brown rice protein is packed with large quantities of absorbable nutrients in an easily digestible form. Sprouting grains converts much of the carbohydrate content into amino acids and denatures enzyme inhibitors. It's very worthwhile to find a sprouted brown rice protein powder rather than settle for a generic one that won't deliver much nutrition. The same goes for nuts and seeds. Soak them whenever you can to remove enzyme inhibitors, which prevent proper digestion. You can even find sprouted nut butters online and in specialty stores.

A'lotta Colada Smoothie

Smooth coconut and the sweet acid flavor of pineapple create a classic piña colada base for this green protein smoothie.

Yield:	Prep time:	Serving size:
about 4 cups	15 minutes	2 cups

Each serving has:		
344 calories	74 g carbohydrate	4 g fat
12 g fiber	11 g protein	

Water and meat of 1 young coconut

2 cups chopped pineapple

1 large fresh banana, peeled

2 large pitted dates

⅛ cup hemp protein powder

5 kale leaves, stems removed

1. In a high-speed blender, combine coconut water and meat, pineapple, banana, dates, hemp protein powder, and kale leaves.

2. Blend until completely smooth.

Variation: Enhance the creamy texture of this smoothie by adding ¼ cup hemp seeds and omitting the hemp protein powder.

Clean Energy Smoothie

The full-bodied marzipan-like flavor of pistachios settles the intensity of wheatgrass while dates sweeten this earthy blend.

Yield:	Prep time:	Serving size:
about 4 cups	15 minutes	2 cups

Each serving has:		
449 calories	53 g carbohydrate	19 g fat
9 g fiber	24 g protein	

⅓ cup pistachio nuts

¼ cup fresh wheatgrass juice

4 large pitted dates

1 cup chopped celery

⅛ cup sprouted brown rice protein powder

1 cup fresh spinach

2 cups water

1. In a high-speed blender, combine pistachio nuts, wheatgrass juice, dates, celery, sprouted brown rice protein powder, spinach, and water.

2. Blend until completely smooth.

Variation: Omit 1 cup water and wheatgrass juice and replace them with 1 cup fresh carrot juice for a flavor that brings out the unique taste of pistachios.

TO YOUR HEALTH!

This smoothie will literally get you running on clean energy! Wheatgrass charges up this electrolyte-rich smoothie alongside easily digested sprouted brown rice protein. In fact, this smoothie is the perfect preworkout drink for the hot yoga fan. It has minerals to keep you in balance and alkalizes your body, priming you to stretch deeply and move with exacting strength.

Cacao Kapow Smoothie!

This smoothie is decadently smooth with a rich chocolate flavor that rivals any traditional chocolate shake. It also has a malty flavor to complement the sweet, nutrient-dense goodness.

Yield:	Prep time:	Serving size:
about 4 cups	15 minutes	2 cups

Each serving has:		
661 calories	82 g carbohydrate	32 g fat
19 g fiber	24 g protein	

2½ cups Brazil nut milk

2 large fresh bananas, peeled

2 large pitted dates

⅛ cup maca powder

⅛ cup mesquite powder

¼ cup raw cacao powder

⅛ cup Brazil nut protein powder

2 cups fresh spinach

1. In a high-speed blender, combine Brazil nut milk, bananas, dates, maca powder, mesquite powder, raw cacao powder, Brazil nut protein powder, and spinach.

2. Blend until completely smooth.

Variation: You can use carob powder instead of mesquite powder in this recipe without sacrificing any of the flavor or nutrition. Almond milk works equally as well for a base in place of Brazil nut milk. Use these variations together to make a **Creamy Carob Smoothie.**

Pumpin' Pumpkin Smoothie

Thick and full-bodied, this smoothie has the floral and citrus notes of apricot and the mild, nutty, and earthy flavor of pumpkin seeds.

Yield:	Prep time:	Serving size:
about 4 cups	15 minutes, plus 1 hour soak time	2 cups

Each serving has:		
628 calories	60 g carbohydrate	33 g fat
10 g fiber	35 g protein	

Heaping ⅔ cup pumpkin seeds	3 kale leaves, stems removed
10 dried apricots	⅛ cup *pea protein powder*
½ cup apricot soak water	1½ cups water
2 cups chopped celery	

1. Soak pumpkin seeds in water to cover for at least 1 hour. Drain and rinse.

2. Soak apricots in water to cover for at least 1 hour. Retain soak water.

3. In a high-speed blender, combine soaked pumpkin seeds, rehydrated apricots, apricot soak water, celery, kale leaves, pea protein powder, and water.

4. Blend until completely smooth.

Variation: Dried apricots are easy to find all year round, so for a seasonal variation, omit 5 apricots and ½ cup water and replace with 2 cups chopped fresh peaches, nectarines, or apricots.

DEFINITION

Pea protein powder is made from yellow split peas and is a nice alternative to other protein powders. It has 25 grams protein in a 1-ounce serving, making it a very viable option for a high-quality protein source. I recommend reading several reviews before purchasing a pea protein powder to be sure you find one with a mild flavor.

Sunflower Salutation Smoothie

Sweet figs give a depth to the mildly sweet flavor of blueberries and add a rich texture to this chocolaty green smoothie.

Yield:	Prep time:	Serving size:
about 4 cups	15 minutes, plus 1 hour soak time	2 cups

Each serving has:		
551 calories	64 g carbohydrate	30 g fat
18 g fiber	18 g protein	

Heaping ⅓ cup sunflower seeds

⅛ cup flaxseeds

6 dried figs

1 large pitted date

1 cup fresh or frozen blueberries

⅛ cup raw cacao powder

5 kale leaves, stems removed

1½ cups water

1. Soak sunflower seeds in water to cover for a minimum of 1 hour. Drain and rinse.

2. In a high-speed blender, combine soaked sunflower seeds, flaxseeds, figs, date, blueberries, raw cacao powder, kale leaves, and water.

3. Blend until completely smooth.

Variation: For a **Sunny Blues Smoothie,** omit the raw cacao powder and use ¼ cup lucuma powder instead. Add 1 cup fresh figs, omit the dried figs, and add 2 additional dates.

Mega Matcha Smoothie

The delicate, sweet smoothness of the cashew milk base lends itself well to the mildly astringent taste of green tea matcha, which is complemented by the subtle savory taste of spirulina in this earthy energy-booster. Chia seeds give this smoothie a texture similar to a bubble tea or tapioca.

Yield:	Prep time:	Serving size:
about 4 cups	30 minutes	2 cups
Each serving has:		
641 calories	83 g carbohydrate	28 g fat
18 g fiber	28 g protein	

2½ cups cashew milk	⅛ cup sprouted brown rice protein powder
1 TB. matcha powder	
2 tsp. spirulina	2 cups fresh spinach
6 large pitted dates	¼ cup chia seeds

1. In a high-speed blender, combine cashew milk, matcha powder, spirulina, dates, sprouted brown rice protein powder, and spinach.

2. Blend until completely smooth.

3. Combine chia seeds with blended smoothie, and stir by hand.

4. Let stand for 10 to 15 minutes for chia seeds to gel.

Variation: Replacing the cashew milk with ¼ cup hemp seeds and 2½ cups water works equally as well as a base to this smoothie. For a more pure matcha taste experience, you may also omit spirulina.

TO YOUR HEALTH!

Need an extra energy boost to get motivated for a day of strenuous activity? You can rely on the smooth surge of energy you'll get from natural green tea powder. Vitamins, minerals, phytonutrients, and plenty of carbs and protein back up the initial energy high of matcha by providing you with sustained energy. This green smoothie alternative to a latte gives you all the motivation you need to get up and running!

Sunflower Power Smoothie

This thick smoothie has a sweet and simple flavor and will make you feel powered up. The slight nuttiness of sunflower seeds is complemented nicely by the deep berry taste of goji berries.

Yield:	Prep time:	Serving size:
about 4 cups	15 minutes, plus 4 hours soak time	2 cups

Each serving has:		
562 calories	78 g carbohydrate	20 g fat
12 g fiber	25 g protein	

Heaping ½ cup sunflower seeds	2 TB. maca powder
¼ cup goji berries	1 cup chopped celery
4 large pitted dates	2 cups fresh spinach
⅛ cup sprouted brown rice protein powder	2 cups water

1. Soak sunflower seeds in water to cover for a minimum of 4 hours. Discard soak water.

2. In a high-speed blender, combine soaked sunflower seeds, goji berries, dates, sprouted brown rice protein powder, maca powder, celery, spinach, and water.

3. Blend until completely smooth.

Variation: For added omega-3s and a different protein spectrum, use ¼ cup hemp seeds and omit ⅓ cup soaked sunflower seeds in this recipe.

Pumping Iron Smoothie

In this wonderfully complex-tasting smoothie, juicy cherries meld nicely with the sweetness of wheatgrass and earthy beet juice to provide a sweet and creamy way to dose up on body-building iron.

Yield:	Prep time:	Serving size:
about 4 cups	15 minutes	2 cups

Each serving has:		
587 calories	84 g carbohydrate	21 g fat
9 g fiber	23 g protein	

1 cup fresh or frozen cherries	4 large pitted dates
⅛ cup fresh wheatgrass juice	4 kale leaves, stems removed
½ cup fresh beet juice	1 cup water
⅓ cup hemp seeds	

1. In a high-speed blender, combine cherries, wheatgrass juice, beet juice, hemp seeds, dates, kale leaves, and water.

2. Blend until completely smooth.

Variation: For a milder-tasting smoothie, replace the wheatgrass juice with 1 teaspoon spirulina.

FRESH FACT

Iron is an essential mineral that can often be lacking in vegetarian diets. Iron binds oxygen for transport to the entire body, and low levels of iron cause extreme fatigue and easy bruising. Without the iron in red blood cells, there'd be nothing for oxygen to attach to. One serving of this Pumping Iron Smoothie provides half of your body's daily requirements for iron.

Super Sesame Smoothie

Sesame is earthy and slightly bitter when compared to other seeds, but it works so nicely with fresh peaches and the sweetness of dried apricots. Carrot juice's deep, sweet flavor rounds out this incredible combination.

Yield:	Prep time:	Serving size:
about 4 cups	15 minutes, plus 1 hour soak time	2 cups

Each serving has:		
454 calories	57 g carbohydrate	21 g fat
13 g fiber	20 g protein	

½ cup unhulled sesame seeds	3 kale leaves, stems removed
6 dried apricots	1 cup fresh carrot juice
⅛ cup hemp protein powder	
2½ cups fresh or frozen chopped peaches	

1. Soak unhulled sesame seeds in water to cover for a minimum of 1 hour. Discard soak water.

2. Soak apricots in water to cover for at least 1 hour.

3. In a high-speed blender, combine soaked sesame seeds, hemp protein powder, peaches, soaked apricots, kale leaves, carrot juice, and apricot soak water.

4. Blend until completely smooth.

Variation: For a milder-tasting smoothie, replace the kale leaves with 2 cups fresh spinach.

Hemp Hummer Smoothie

Bananas and spirulina have a great flavor affinity. Spirulina brings a salty taste that helps balance the sweetness of the bananas and figs and blends perfectly with the malty, pungent taste of maca and nutty hemp seeds.

Yield:	Prep time:	Serving size:
about 4 cups	15 minutes	2 cups
Each serving has:		
471 calories	56 g carbohydrate	20 g fat
8 g fiber	22 g protein	

⅓ cup hemp seeds

2 medium fresh bananas, peeled

4 dried figs

⅛ cup maca powder

1 TB. spirulina

4 kale leaves, stems removed

1½ cups water

1. In a high-speed blender, combine hemp seeds, bananas, figs, maca powder, spirulina, kale leaves, and water.

2. Blend until completely smooth.

Variation: For an added protein boost, add 2 tablespoons hemp protein powder to this well-balanced smoothie.

TO YOUR HEALTH!

Of all the high-protein plant foods, hemp seeds and spirulina are the easiest to digest. This really makes the Hemp Hummer Smoothie ideal to drink when you need energy and nutrition *now!*

Charged Up Chia Smoothie

This smoothie is all mild and sweet creaminess with a fun tapioca-like texture from the chia seeds. The smoothie base is on the thinner side and is bulked up by adding chia.

Yield:	Prep time:	Serving size:
about 4 cups	15 minutes, plus 1 hour soak time	2 cups

Each serving has:		
1,085 calories	136 g carbohydrate	54 g fat
33 g fiber	26 g protein	

6 dried figs	⅛ cup hemp protein powder
2½ cups Brazil nut milk	3 cups fresh spinach
1 cup goji berries	¼ cup chia seeds

1. Soak figs in water to cover for at least 1 hour. Discard soak water.

2. In a high-speed blender, combine Brazil nut milk, goji berries, hemp protein powder, soaked figs, and spinach.

3. Blend until completely smooth.

4. Add chia seeds to smoothie, and stir by hand.

5. Let stand for 10 to 15 minutes before drinking to allow chia seeds to gel.

Variation: Brazil nut milk is used here for its high protein content, but feel free to substitute any other nut milk instead.

Macho Mango Smoothie

This smoothie may taste fruity and floral, and it may be creamy and silky, but it still packs a macho amount of nutrition!

Yield:	Prep time:	Serving size:
about 4 cups	15 minutes, plus 1 hour soak time	2 cups

Each serving has:		
379 calories	33 g carbohydrate	21 g fat
6 g fiber	19 g protein	

3 dried apricots	2 TB. fresh lemon juice
1½ cups chopped mango	1½ cups water (including soak water)
⅓ cup hemp seeds	
3 cups fresh spinach	

1. Soak apricots in water to cover for at least 1 hour. Drain, retaining soak water.

2. In a high-speed blender, combine mango, hemp seeds, soaked apricots, spinach, lemon juice, and water.

3. Blend until completely smooth.

Variation: Substitute ⅓ cup pistachios for hemp seeds for a totally different flavor.

TO YOUR HEALTH!

Mango has a very exotic taste and isn't generally associated with protein drinks or green smoothies, but this smoothie will take your workout to the tropics!

Pump-kin Up! Smoothie

This is an incredibly thick smoothie that's very sweet, simple, and earthy tasting.

Yield:	Prep time:	Serving size:
about 4 cups	15 minutes, plus 1 hour soak time	2 cups

Each serving has:		
559 calories	71 g carbohydrate	25 g fat
12 g fiber	25 g protein	

Heaping ½ cup pumpkin seeds	1 TB. ginseng powder
⅛ cup hemp protein powder	6 kale leaves, stems removed
2 large pitted dates	1 cup water
2 large fresh bananas, peeled	

1. Soak pumpkin seeds in water to cover for at least 1 hour. Drain and discard soak water.

2. In a high-speed blender, combine soaked pumpkin seeds, hemp protein powder, dates, bananas, ginseng powder, kale leaves, and water.

3. Blend until completely smooth.

Variation: This is a very sweet smoothie. If you prefer to tone down the sweetness, omit the dates.

Kid-Friendly Smoothies

Chapter 10

In This Chapter

- Kid-friendly health food
- Teaching kids that *healthy* means "great tasting"
- Parents as healthy role models
- Kid-approved green smoothies

Smoothies are generally very kid friendly because they're sweet and creamy and full of delicious fruit. Fresh green smoothies are not such a deviation from fruit smoothies as you might think. There are plenty of ways to make greens appealing to children, and I think green smoothies are the easiest method. Serving green smoothies to children is a perfect way to sneak leafy greens and superfoods into their diets and ensure they're getting the nutrition they need.

Because kids can be finicky when it comes to food, the smoothie recipes in this chapter contain fewer greens than the ones in other chapters. This is done intentionally with the idea that it's better to get their taste buds acclimated to greens as they begin to enjoy the healthy flavors and taste. We want to get kids hooked on greens for life! You can always add more greens to these smoothie recipes as your child becomes more accustomed to flavors and appreciative of the taste.

The smoothies in this chapter are aimed at helping parents build a repertoire of healthy whole food drinks your kids—and you!—will love. Becoming familiar with these recipes will teach you the basics about how to create flavor combinations kids will ask for over and over again.

Shifting the Paradigm

In general, people like foods that appeal to their taste buds. Children are certainly no exception to this rule and tend to be even more insistent than adults about only eating foods that are pleasing to their palate. When children decide they don't like something, they may never try it again. For some, this rejection can span nearly the entire vegetable kingdom.

The funny thing is that healthy food *does* taste good. Most people who say otherwise have merely eaten ill-prepared food, are addicted to flavor enhancers, or have been told by an adult that it tastes bad. Fresh fruit seems to be the exception to this generality, which makes it the perfect delivery system for shifting the "healthy food tastes bad" paradigm.

Green smoothies don't just taste like vegetables; they include flavors and textures kids like and provide a wonderful vehicle for nutrition. Just getting kids over the idea that *healthy food* means "bad tasting" can be one of the more difficult challenges and one of the most important notions to change. Thankfully, many times children seem to gravitate to these great-tasting smoothies.

Introducing Your Kids to Green Smoothies

Because processed foods can be addicting, sometimes children express resistance to major dietary changes. If they have taste aversions to green smoothies, you can change this by simply preparing some of these wonderful recipes for them.

An easy way to begin adding green smoothies into a child's everyday diet is to serve it as a side to an otherwise familiar breakfast. Increase the serving each day over a period of 2 weeks until the smoothie replaces the other food.

Another way to introduce smoothies as a main source of nourishment is to remove the worst aspects of the diet several weeks prior to introducing green smoothies. Using this method, there won't be such a strong reaction, leaving less of a chance for aversions to develop.

You can also try making a smoothie from the recipe section using fewer greens than what's called for. If your child likes it, you can increase the amount of greens over time.

FRESH FACT

Your child loves you and learns from the examples set by you and other family members. Often, children will gravitate toward the food their parents or siblings eat, especially if they know some foods are restricted or off limits. If you, as the parent, drink green smoothies, your children will eventually get curious. Don't worry about *making* your child drink green smoothies. Just make one for yourself and refuse to share it for a while until your child decides he or she *must* have it!

You may have to take a more intellectual approach with older children and teenagers. Just explain the benefits of drinking green smoothies. That's often enough to convince a preteen to give it a go. Tell your teenager that drinking lots of green smoothies will help clear up acne and keep them slim. When they see the benefits, they'll be lifelong converts.

Whatever approach you decide to take, keep in mind that the best way to convince any resistant child to try something new is to give them a lot of space and freedom when making a decision about whether or not to give it a go.

Red Velvet Smoothie

Chocolate and strawberries make a rich and flavorful combination that adds a fruity twist to the mild cocoa taste. Hemp makes it pleasantly creamy, and grass powder adds a malty flavor. This smoothie is sweet enough your kids won't notice the greens.

Yield:	Prep time:	Serving size:
about 4 cups	15 minutes	2 cups

Each serving has:		
425 calories	60 g carbohydrate	15 g fat
12 g fiber	17 g protein	

1 cup chopped celery

½ cup water

2 TB. maple syrup

¼ cup hemp seeds

2 cups fresh or frozen strawberries

1 large fresh banana, peeled

1 TB. grass powder, such as dried wheatgrass or barley grass

2 TB. raw cacao powder

2 kale leaves, stems removed

1. In a high-speed blender, combine celery, water, maple syrup, hemp seeds, strawberries, banana, grass powder, raw cacao powder, and kale leaves.

2. Blend until completely smooth.

Variation: Consider adding raspberries, or any other fresh local berry, in place of the strawberries.

FRESH FACT

Food-grade hemp seeds are an incredible source of natural protein; omega-3, -6, and -9; and chlorophyll. They're perfect for children's nutrition because they're nutty and delicious. Hemp provides many beneficial nutrients in the form of essential minerals, vitamins, and many phytonutrients and there's absolutely no trace of THC (tetrahydrocannabinol), the active constituent in the intoxicating marijuana plant.

Almond Milkshake Smoothie

Almost like a vanilla milkshake, this smoothie is sweet, creamy, and thick.

Yield:	Prep time:	Serving size:
about 4 cups	15 minutes	2 cups
Each serving has:		
465 calories	60 g carbohydrate	25 g fat
8 g fiber	9 g protein	

1 cup chopped celery

1½ cups water

⅓ cup almond butter

2 tsp. spirulina, chlorella, or *AFA blue-green algae*

2 large peeled and frozen bananas

2 large pitted dates

1 cup fresh spinach

1. In a high-speed blender, combine celery, water, almond butter, spirulina, bananas, dates, and spinach.

2. Blend until completely smooth.

Variation: Make this drink even more nutrition packed by using sesame seed butter (tahini) in place of the almond butter. You can also replace the bananas and dates with about 10 dried figs.

> **DEFINITION**
>
> **AFA (aphanizomenon flos-aquae) blue-green algae** is a cyanobacteria commonly known as a blue-green algae. It's a high-quality source of amino acids, phycocyanin, phenylethylamine, polysaccharides, essential fatty acids such as EPA and DHA, and nearly every necessary vitamin and mineral.

Ultra Violet Smoothie

Creamy hemp and chia seeds with perfect blueberries make a wonderful base for the greener things in life. This smoothie is sweet all the way around.

Yield:	Prep time:	Serving size:
about 4 cups	15 minutes	2 cups

Each serving has:		
374 calories	49 g carbohydrate	16 g fat
9 g fiber	15 g protein	

¼ cup hemp seeds	1 tsp. spirulina
1 TB. chia seeds	1½ cups water
2 TB. maple syrup	1 large fresh banana, peeled
1½ cups fresh or frozen blueberries	3 kale leaves, stems removed

1. In a high-speed blender, combine hemp seeds, chia seeds, maple syrup, blueberries, spirulina, water, banana, and kale leaves.

2. Blend until completely smooth.

Variation: For an even more exciting and exotic twist on this smoothie, replace the blueberries with black raspberries.

TO YOUR HEALTH!

The brilliant dark violet color will be enough to get your little one excited about this smoothie! Packed with equal parts super nutrition and great taste, it boasts high-quality protein and a full spectrum of vitamins and minerals. It's great for adults, too!

Coco Colada Smoothie

Mild spinach is barely noticeable when combined with sweet dates and syrupy pineapple in this smoothie.

Yield:	Prep time:	Serving size:
about 4 cups	15 minutes	2 cups

Each serving has:		
286 calories	70 g carbohydrate	2 g fat
6 g fiber	4 g protein	

Water and meat of 1 young coconut

1 large peeled and frozen banana

2 cups fresh or frozen chopped pineapple

2 large pitted dates

2 cups fresh spinach

1. In a high-speed blender, combine coconut water and meat, banana, pineapple, dates, and spinach.

2. Blend until completely smooth.

Variation: If you can't find young coconut, you may use 1½ cups ready-to-drink unsweetened coconut milk. Or you may omit the banana and add 1 whole or peeled kiwi instead.

Orange Cream Smoothie

Tart *camu camu berry* enhances the citrus element in this creamy orange smoothie. The apricots bring a sweetness to the mix and add a mildly floral note.

Yield:	Prep time:	Serving size:
about 4 cups	15 minutes	2 cups

Each serving has:		
356 calories	54 g carbohydrate	15 g fat
8 g fiber	9 g protein	

2 oranges, peeled, seeded, and sectioned

1 large fresh banana, peeled

¼ cup cashew butter or ½ cup cashews

1 TB. camu camu powder

5 dried apricots

½ cup water

2 cups fresh sorrel

1. In a high-speed blender, combine oranges, banana, cashew butter, camu camu powder, apricots, water, and sorrel.

2. Blend until completely smooth.

Variation: If you want to add a calcium boost, replace the dried apricots with 8 dried figs.

DEFINITION

The **camu camu berry** is a grape-size berry from the Amazon Basin that boasts a higher vitamin C content than any other known plant. It's reputed to increase serotonin levels, which can have mood-balancing effects. It has antiviral and antiseptic properties that make it a useful immunity booster, too.

Chocolate Hazelnut Smoothie

Chocolate hazelnut fans rejoice! This is a fresh take on a favorite sweet combination with added nutrition.

Yield:	Prep time:	Serving size:
about 4 cups	15 minutes	2 cups

Each serving has:		
607 calories	80 g carbohydrate	30 g fat
14 g fiber	13 g protein	

2 medium fresh bananas, peeled

⅓ cup hazelnut butter

4 large pitted dates

¼ cup raw cacao powder

1½ cups water

2 cups fresh spinach

1. In a high-speed blender, combine bananas, hazelnut butter, dates, raw cacao powder, water, and spinach.

2. Blend until completely smooth.

Variation: This smoothie is wonderful on its own or can be enhanced by replacing the water with orange juice and adding 1 teaspoon orange zest.

FRESH FACT

Hazelnuts are a protein-rich nut and contain high levels of the antioxidant vitamin E. Their fat composition is similar to that of olive oil, making them very heart healthy.

Perfect Purple Smoothie

The beautiful color the beets bring to this smoothie will be enough to convince children to drink their veggies. The sweet, clean taste will make them glad they did!

Yield:	Prep time:	Serving size:
about 4 cups	15 minutes	2 cups

Each serving has:		
130 calories	31 g carbohydrate	1 g fat
6 g fiber	4 g protein	

½ cup fresh beet juice

2 cups chopped apple (your favorite)

2 cups chopped celery

3 kale leaves, stems removed

1 cup water

1. In a high-speed blender, combine beet juice, apple, celery, kale leaves, and water.

2. Blend until completely smooth.

Variation: Add ⅛ cup lemon juice for a more tart smoothie.

Raspberry Zing Smoothie

Tart and sweet in all the right places, the pineapple and raspberry in this smoothie play well together while mild spinach adds to the overall pleasing taste.

Yield:	Prep time:	Serving size:
about 4 cups	15 minutes	2 cups
Each serving has:		
186 calories	46 g carbohydrate	1 g fat
11 g fiber	3 g protein	

2 cups chopped fresh pineapple	½ cup water
2 cups fresh or frozen raspberries	2 TB. maple syrup
	1 cup fresh spinach

1. In a high-speed blender, combine pineapple, raspberries, water, maple syrup, and spinach.

2. Blend until completely smooth.

Variation: For a creamy smoothie, omit the water and add the water and meat of 1 young coconut.

BLENDER BLUNDER

If you're using a whole pineapple in this recipe, be sure to remove the pineapple's "eyes" to ensure a smooth blend. You should also remove the pineapple's core, which tastes very acidic.

Green Lemonade Smoothie

What kid doesn't like colorful lemonade? Give them a fun time with this tart, sweet, green drink!

Yield:	Prep time:	Serving size:
about 4 cups	15 minutes	2 cups

Each serving has:		
265 calories	70 g carbohydrate	1 g fat
6 g fiber	5 g protein	

¾ cup fresh lemon juice

6 large pitted dates

2 cups celery juice

2 cups fresh spinach

1. In a high-speed blender, combine lemon juice, dates, celery juice, and spinach.

2. Blend until completely smooth.

Variation: You can also add ¼ cup wheatgrass juice and ½ cup water in place of the spinach.

Banana Berry Smoothie

This beautiful purple smoothie is sweet berry heaven.

Yield:	Prep time:	Serving size:
about 4 cups	15 minutes	2 cups

Each serving has:		
434 calories	56 g carbohydrate	17 g fat
14 g fiber	10 g protein	

2 cups hazelnut milk	1 large fresh banana, peeled
1½ cups fresh or frozen blackberries	2 large pitted dates
	3 kale leaves, stems removed

1. In a high-speed blender, combine hazelnut milk, blackberries, banana, pitted dates, and kale leaves.

2. Blend until completely smooth.

Variation: Use black raspberries to replace blackberries in this smoothie. You will get a wonderful, almost perfumelike flavor.

FRESH FACT

Antioxidant-packed blackberries are a great way to diversify your child's nutrition. They'll love the color and the taste of this great purple and green smoothie.

Mango Monkey Smoothie

Smooth and luscious mango, warm floral vanilla, and creamy Brazil nut milk make a refreshing and nourishing smoothie any mango fan will love!

Yield:	Prep time:	Serving size:
about 4 cups	15 minutes	2 cups

Each serving has:		
428 calories	45 g carbohydrate	28 g fat
7 g fiber	8 g protein	

2 cups Brazil nut milk

1½ cups chopped fresh ripe mango

2 large pitted dates

1½ cups fresh spinach

1 tsp. vanilla extract

1. In a high-speed blender, combine Brazil nut milk, mango, dates, spinach, and vanilla extract.

2. Blend until completely smooth.

Variation: For a berry-filled **Blue Monkey Smoothie,** replace the mango with 1½ cups fresh or frozen blueberries and 2 more dates.

Mint Cookies 'N' Cream Smoothie

There may be no cookies in this decadent smoothie, but the mint chocolaty flavor and rich creaminess will keep your kids wanting more.

Yield:	Prep time:	Serving size:
about 4 cups	15 minutes	2 cups
Each serving has:		
703 calories	99 g carbohydrate	32 g fat
26 g fiber	17 g protein	

½ cup macadamia nuts

½ cup raw cacao powder

6 large pitted dates

¾ cup fresh mint leaves

1 cup fresh spinach

1 tsp. vanilla extract

2 cups water

1. In a high-speed blender, combine macadamia nuts, raw cacao powder, dates, mint leaves, spinach, vanilla extract, and water.

2. Blend until completely smooth.

Variation: If you prefer, replace the water and macadamia nuts with 3 cups almond milk.

TO YOUR HEALTH!

Sometimes all it takes to get kids to eat healthy is providing them a healthy twist on something they already know and like. But hey, if your kids still need a bit of convincing before giving green smoothies a try, you can always serve this smoothie with an organic sandwich cookie on the side for some extra motivation!

Berry Vanilla Smoothie

Subtle blueberries and sweet but tart raspberries and blackberries are blended into creamy berry bliss when combined with floral yet earthy vanilla.

Yield:	Prep time:	Serving size:
about 4 cups	15 minutes	2 cups
Each serving has:		
467 calories	81 g carbohydrate	18 g fat
12 g fiber	8 g protein	

1½ cups almond milk	½ cup fresh or frozen raspberries
1 cup fresh or frozen blueberries	5 large pitted dates
½ cup fresh or frozen blackberries	2 kale leaves, stems removed
	2 tsp. vanilla extract

1. In a high-speed blender, combine almond milk, blueberries, blackberries, raspberries, dates, kale leaves, and vanilla extract.

2. Blend until completely smooth.

Variation: Try replacing blueberries in this recipe with 2 packets frozen acai for a berry taste that perfectly complements the vanilla extract.

Chocolate Cherry Smoothie

The unmistakable sweetness of cherries and the rich flavor of chocolate come together for a decadent treat. Almond butter gives this smoothie a luscious texture and adds depth to the flavor. A perfect drink for both kids and adults!

Yield:	Prep time:	Serving size:
about 4 cups	15 minutes	2 cups

Each serving has:		
793 calories	140 g carbohydrate	23 g fat
26 g fiber	20 g protein	

¼ cup almond butter	1½ cups fresh or frozen cherries
½ cup raw cacao powder	1 cup fresh spinach
6 large pitted dates	1 cup water

1. In a high-speed blender, combine almond butter, raw cacao powder, dates, cherries, spinach, and water.

2. Blend until completely smooth.

Variation: For extra nutrition and health benefits, add ½ cup goji berries to this smoothie.

FRESH FACT

Cherries are rich in fiber and iron—two things most kids need more of. This smoothie might seem like a sweet treat, but it has great nutritional benefits that make it worth its weight in broccoli.

Pineapple Punch Smoothie

Tart and tangy pineapple combines with a big berry flavor to bring in the healthy greens.

Yield:	Prep time:	Serving size:
about 4 cups	15 minutes	2 cups

Each serving has:		
229 calories	57 g carbohydrate	1 g fat
10 g fiber	5 g protein	

1 cup chopped fresh pineapple	1 TB. fresh lemon juice
1 cup fresh or frozen strawberries	2 large pitted dates
½ cup fresh or frozen raspberries	1 cup fresh celery juice
½ cup fresh or frozen blueberries	2 kale leaves, stems removed

1. In a high-speed blender, combine pineapple, strawberries, raspberries, blueberries, lemon juice, dates, celery juice, and kale leaves.

2. Blend until completely smooth.

Variation: You may use any berries or sweet fruit you like in this smoothie, depending on what's available and what you like. Try replacing strawberries with 1 cup chopped mango, for example.

Strawberries 'N' Cream Smoothie

Whip goji berries and strawberries into a beautiful pink, frothy, and creamy smoothie with hints of vanilla and just a touch of lemon to enhance the strawberry flavor.

Yield:	Prep time:	Serving size:
about 4 cups	15 minutes	2 cups
Each serving has:		
533 calories	99 g carbohydrate	16 g fat
12 g fiber	9 g protein	

1½ cups cashew milk

2 cups fresh or frozen strawberries

¼ cup goji berries

2 tsp. fresh lemon juice

6 large pitted dates

1 cup fresh spinach

1 tsp. vanilla extract

1. In a high-speed blender, combine cashew milk, strawberries, goji berries, lemon juice, dates, spinach, and vanilla extract.

2. Blend until completely smooth.

Variation: For a **Strawberry Lemonade Smoothie,** omit the vanilla extract and cashew milk, and add 1 cup water and an additional ½ cup lemon juice instead.

BLENDER BLUNDER

Take care not to add more than the recommended amount of lemon juice to this smoothie or it will upset the flavor balance. Lemon is used here to enhance the flavor of the strawberries but could easily overpower the drink if too much is added.

Exotic Green Smoothies

In This Chapter

- Using exotic ingredients
- Exciting flavor combinations
- Exotic green smoothies

Exotic fruits, nuts, seeds, spices, and herbs are the perfect way to jazz up your green smoothie menu and give your body a chance to acquire nutrients that may be lacking in your diet.

It can also be exciting to experiment with the traditional drinks and unique flavors commonly used in other regions. You'll certainly be surprised by the ways these traditional flavors can be enhanced by turning them into delicious green smoothies.

The bright, bold, floral, and rich flavors of the exotic green smoothies in this chapter will give you new ideas for flavor combinations and ways to use ethnic ingredients.

Hawaiian Pineapple Guava Smoothie

The sweet and tart flavors of guava and pineapple have subtle similarities, yet both are incredibly distinct. Guava, in particular, has a wonderful floral, berrylike flavor. Creamy coconut blends this combination into a tropical taste experience.

Yield:	Prep time:	Serving size:
about 4 cups	15 minutes	2 cups

Each serving has:		
244 calories	58 g carbohydrate	3 g fat
12 g fiber	3 g protein	

2 cups chopped strawberry guava	Water and meat of 1 young coconut
1 cup chopped pineapple	2 cups fresh spinach

1. In a high-speed blender, combine strawberry guava, pineapple, coconut water and meat, and spinach.

2. Blend until completely smooth.

Variation: Strawberry guava is a common, commercially produced variety, but you may use any other guava you prefer. If you live in the Pacific Northwest, you may be able to easily acquire pineapple guava (feijoa). Use these interchangeably with strawberry guava.

German Nettle Mint Smoothie

Bright mint, mild nettle, and the licorice-like taste of anise are enhanced by sweet apple and tart currant. Asparagus adds a pleasant, mild savory balance to this refreshing smoothie.

Yield:	Prep time:	Serving size:
about 4 cups	15 minutes	2 cups
Each serving has:		
172 calories	42 g carbohydrate	1 g fat
11 g fiber	4 g protein	

3 cups chopped apple (your favorite)

3 small asparagus spears, chopped

½ cup fresh currants

1 tsp. anise seeds

2 cups chopped nettle

1 cup fresh mint leaves

1 cup water

1. In a high-speed blender, combine apple, asparagus, currants, anise seeds, nettle, mint leaves, and water.

2. Blend until completely smooth.

Variation: As a variation, omit the asparagus and currants, and add 1 cup chopped fennel instead. Or use another local wild green such as purslane or lamb's quarters if nettle isn't in season.

 FRESH FACT

A green smoothie probably isn't the first thing you think of when German cuisine—normally heavy and rich—is mentioned. But keep an open mind because many fruits and vegetables are common to German cooking and perfect for smoothies. Several of these ingredients have been specially selected and combined into this powerful and flavorful smoothie.

Mesoamerican Sapote Smoothie

Sapote is a sweet fruit that's creamy like a banana but with a more custardlike texture. This simple smoothie stays true to the pure creaminess and pleasant flavor of sapote by adding just a bit of mild-tasting spinach.

Yield:	Prep time:	Serving size:
about 4 cups	15 minutes	2 cups

Each serving has:		
133 calories	32 g carbohydrate	1 g fat
5 g fiber	2 g protein	

2½ cups sapote, seeds removed   1½ cups Brazil nut milk

2 cups fresh spinach

1. In a high-speed blender, combine sapote, spinach, and Brazil nut milk.

2. Blend until completely smooth.

FRESH FACT

The only nut that's native to Mesoamerica is the Ramon nut, which is not widely distributed on the international market. However, if you come across Ramon nuts, you can use them to make a nut milk to use in place of the Brazil nut milk in this recipe.

Mexican Prickly Pear Smoothie

Prickly pear is a very juicy and mild sweet fruit. It's a perfect companion to cooling cucumber, zesty watercress, spicy jalapeño, and tart lime juice.

Yield:	Prep time:	Serving size:
about 4 cups	20 minutes	2 cups

Each serving has:		
109 calories	25 g carbohydrate	1 g fat
9 g fiber	3 g protein	

4 medium prickly pears	1 cup fresh spinach
⅛ cup fresh lime juice	1 TB. diced fresh jalapeño (or your favorite pepper)
1 cup chopped cucumber	
1 small bunch watercress	1 cup water

1. If your prickly pears contain seeds throughout, peel prickly pears, place in a food processor, and pulse lightly a few times until fruits release their liquid but seeds are still whole.

2. Press processed prickly pears through a large mesh strainer or colander to remove seeds.

3. In a high-speed blender, combine prickly pears, lime juice, cucumber, watercress, spinach, jalapeño, and water.

4. Blend until completely smooth.

Variation: For a slightly sweeter blend, omit the lime juice and add 1 large pitted date.

BLENDER BLUNDER

Handle prickly pears with care! Wild-crafted varieties have long spines that grow in clusters and less-obvious hairlike prickly fuzz that can imbed in your skin. Many store-bought varieties are free of these hairs, but if you're picking wild prickly pears, use gloves to handle the prickly pear while cutting it off the cactus. Place the prickly pears in a colander while running water over them, and use a gloved hand to rub the skin and remove the hairs. You can then peel off the skin and eat the fruit whole. The seeds are edible; however, they're very hard and I recommend removing them before blending. Some varieties contain seeds throughout while others have seeds that can be easily scooped out of the center of the fruit.

Mexican Chia Tonic Smoothie

In this incredibly rich and smooth, savory smoothie, tomato, avocado, lime juice, and cilantro combine to provide a wonderful base for the chia seeds and nopal cactus.

Yield:	Prep time:	Serving size:
about 4 cups	15 minutes	2 cups

Each serving has:		
179 calories	26 g carbohydrate	9 g fat
11 g fiber	6 g protein	

¼ cup avocado

⅛ cup chia seeds

1 cup chopped tomato

½ cup filleted nopal cactus

¼ cup fresh lime juice

⅛ cup whole dulse or dulse flakes

1 cup chopped fresh cilantro

1 cup chopped chard leaves

1 cup water

1. In a high-speed blender, combine avocado, chia seeds, tomato, nopal cactus, lime juice, dulse, cilantro, chard leaves, and water.

2. Blend until completely smooth.

Variation: For a **Savory Succulent Smoothie,** replace the tomato with cucumber and the nopal cactus with aloe vera.

Turkish Sesame Rose Smoothie

The enchanting essence of rose is a delightful companion to sweet figs. Earthy and creamy tahini adds an ethereal taste with grounded nutrition.

Yield:	Prep time:	Serving size:
about 4 cups	15 minutes	2 cups
Each serving has:		
457 calories	68 g carbohydrate	21 g fat
11 g fiber	10 g protein	

⅓ cup tahini	3 large pitted dates
¼ cup rose water	2 cups fresh spinach
5 fresh figs	1½ cups water

1. In a high-speed blender, combine tahini, rose water, figs, dates, spinach, and water.

2. Blend until completely smooth.

Variation: For a delectable **Orange Blossom Smoothie,** replace the rose water with neroli water and the fresh figs with fresh apricots.

TO YOUR HEALTH!

This Turkish Sesame Rose Smoothie is a soul-soothing drink perfect for special occasions and is deeply comforting and nourishing. Drink it with intention, and stop to smell the roses.

Eastern Apricot Pistachio Smoothie

Fruity and floral apricot and the creamy taste of pistachio reminiscent of marzipan create a complex counterbalance to the savory sensation of parsley.

Yield:	Prep time:	Serving size:
about 4 cups	15 minutes	2 cups

Each serving has:		
352 calories	41 g carbohydrate	19 g fat
9 g fiber	12 g protein	

⅓ cup pistachios

2½ cups chopped cucumber

10 dried apricots

1 cup chopped fresh parsley

1½ cups water

1. In a high-speed blender, combine pistachios, cucumber, apricots, parsley, and water.

2. Blend until completely smooth.

Variation: Another way to get a wonderful-tasting, exotic blend would be to replace the parsley with fresh spinach.

Indian Mango Lassi Smoothie

Luscious ripe mango with a tart twist reminiscent of yogurt, this smoothie is pure sweet indulgence.

Yield:	Prep time:	Serving size:
about 4 cups	15 minutes	2 cups
Each serving has:		
454 calories	72 g carbohydrate	19 g fat
12 g fiber	9 g protein	

1½ cups chopped mango

2 cups cashew milk (or other nut milk)

1 TB. lemon juice

⅛ cup chia seeds

4 large pitted dates

2 cups fresh spinach

1. In a high-speed blender, combine mango, cashew milk, lemon juice, chia seeds, dates, and spinach.

2. Blend until completely smooth.

Variation: For a more traditional Indian *lassi*, add ⅛ teaspoon cardamom powder and a few sprigs fresh mint.

DEFINITION

A **lassi** is an Indian drink with a taste as rich as the culture it comes from. Traditionally, it's made with a thin yogurt, water or rose water, mango, and sometimes added sugar. In my vegan version, mild-tasting spinach increases the nutritional value.

Indian Mango Mint Smoothie

Fresh, luscious, sweet mango with a tart twist is enveloped by the spicy kick of cayenne and the cooling sensation of mint.

Yield:	Prep time:	Serving size:
about 4 cups	15 minutes	2 cups

Each serving has:		
188 calories	49 g carbohydrate	1 g fat
6 g fiber	2 g protein	

2 cups mango	1 cup fresh spinach
2 large pitted dates	2 TB. fresh lemon juice
1 (2-in.) piece fresh peeled turmeric	¼ tsp. cayenne
1 cup fresh mint leaves	2 cups water

1. In a high-speed blender, combine mango, dates, turmeric, mint leaves, spinach, lemon juice, cayenne, and water.

2. Blend until completely smooth.

Variation: Replace the mango with an equal amount of papaya for an equally sweet and less-tart blend.

Balinese Asam Kunyit Smoothie

Tart tamarind, fresh mint, earthy turmeric, and savory basil combine into a beautiful symphony of herbal power. A touch of honey adds a bit of sweetness and balances the other flavors in this smoothie.

Yield:	Prep time:	Serving size:
about 4 cups	15 minutes	2 cups

Each serving has:		
224 calories	58 g carbohydrate	1 g fat
6 g fiber	3 g protein	

½ cup tamarind paste, seeds removed

2 TB. maple syrup or raw honey

1 (3-in.) piece fresh peeled turmeric

1 TB. fresh lemon juice

1 cup fresh Thai basil leaves

1 cup fresh mint leaves

2½ cups water

1. In a high-speed blender, combine tamarind paste, maple syrup, turmeric, lemon juice, Thai basil leaves, mint leaves, and water.

2. Blend until completely smooth.

Variation: For an extra-powerful drink that's consistent with traditional Balinese folk remedies, add 1 inch fresh peeled ginger and 1 cup chopped fresh cilantro.

BLENDER BLUNDER

I've suggested raw honey as an alternative to maple syrup in this recipe because it's consistent with the traditional Asam Kunyit drink frequently enjoyed in Bali for its health benefits. Please remember that honey is not an appropriate food for children under 1 year old because it may present severe health complications.

Thai Basil Mango Smoothie

This fresh and creamy tropical blend has a sweetness that entices the taste buds and complex herbal flavors to keep your palate engaged and excited.

Yield:	Prep time:	Serving size:
about 4 cups	15 minutes	2 cups

Each serving has:		
219 calories	52 g carbohydrate	2 g fat
5 g fiber	3 g protein	

2½ cups chopped mango

Water and meat of 1 young coconut

½ cup chopped fresh cilantro

1 cup fresh spinach

1 cup fresh Thai basil leaves

⅛ cup fresh lemon juice

1. In a high-speed blender, combine mango, coconut water and meat, cilantro, spinach, Thai basil leaves, and lemon juice.

2. Blend until completely smooth.

Variation: Also consider making this smoothie with pineapple in place of the mango for an exciting flavor zing.

Thai Lychee Lemongrass Smoothie

The flavor of the lychee is similar to a fragrant grape. It creates a mild fruity and floral base that adds character to the bright flavors of lemongrass, cilantro, and subtle hint of mint.

Yield:	Prep time:	Serving size:
about 4 cups	15 minutes	2 cups

Each serving has:		
416 calories	36 g carbohydrate	1 g fat
5g fiber	2g protein	

2 cups peeled and seeded lychees

2 cups chopped celery

⅛ cup fresh lime juice

1 (½-in.) piece fresh peeled ginger

1 cup chopped fresh cilantro

¼ cup fresh mint leaves

2 TB. slivered lemongrass from thick base of stalk

1 cup water

1. In a high-speed blender, combine lychees, celery, lime juice, ginger, cilantro, mint leaves, lemongrass, and water.

2. Blend until completely smooth.

Variation: Try replacing the celery with cucumber and omitting the mint for a pleasant variation.

FRESH FACT

The phenols in the sweet, unassuming lychee fruit are said to improve blood flow to the organs, which is why it's used as a folk remedy for treating the flu. Paired with ginger and fever-fighting lemongrass, this smoothie is a hit for the cold season when you feel like you need a tropical vacation!

Thai Pineapple Ginger Smoothie

Sweet, tart, and savory, this smoothie is mild and intense at the same time. Sweet bell peppers and pineapple are an interesting combination enhanced by the aromatic lemongrass and warming, pungent ginger.

Yield:	Prep time:	Serving size:
about 4 cups	15 minutes	2 cups

Each serving has:		
141 calories	34 g carbohydrate	1 g fat
6 g fiber	3 g protein	

2½ cups chopped pineapple

1 cup chopped orange bell pepper

1 (2-in.) piece fresh peeled ginger

1 TB. slivered lemongrass from thick base of stalk

1 TB. fresh lemon juice

1½ cups fresh chopped cilantro

½ cup fresh Thai basil leaves

1 cup water

1. In a high-speed blender, combine pineapple, orange bell pepper, ginger, lemongrass, lemon juice, cilantro, Thai basil leaves, and water.

2. Blend until completely smooth.

Variation: Try replacing the bell pepper with mango for a sweeter and less-savory smoothie.

Malaysian Mangosteen Smoothie

Mangosteen's incredibly sour and sweet flavor, reminiscent of pineapple and grape, creates an exotic and smooth combination with the distinctive flavor of papaya.

Yield:	Prep time:	Serving size:
about 4 cups	15 minutes	2 cups

Each serving has:		
133 calories	32 g carbohydrate	1 g fat
5 g fiber	2 g protein	

1 cup fresh peeled and seeded mangosteen	2 cups fresh spinach
2 cups chopped ripe papaya	1½ cups water

1. In a high-speed blender, combine mangosteen, papaya, spinach, and water.

2. Blend until completely smooth.

Variation: Cherimoya has a flavor similar to that of mangosteen, yet is creamy like a banana. Depending on the season, it may be easier to find cherimoya than mangosteen. To substitute, add 1 cup cherimoya in place of the mangosteen.

TO YOUR HEALTH!

Mangosteen is a fruit renowned in the superfood and natural healing circles. With its fragrant, slightly floral, sweet-and-sour flavor, it's certainly a fruit you'll remember eating. You may also want to blend part or all of the rind, which has a bitter taste but is very antioxidant rich. The outer rind is tough once it dries, and the easiest way to access the fruit is by using a pairing knife to make a shallow cut around the center of the fruit. Then twist the fruit open and gently scoop out the white fruit. You may eat the seeds or discard them.

Indonesian Durian Smoothie

Durian is sweet, creamy, and very pungent. Coconut water and meat really tone down the flavor of durian, and spinach makes this blend a perfect complex yet simple-tasting custardlike smoothie.

Yield:	Prep time:	Serving size:
about 4 cups	15 minutes	2 cups

Each serving has:		
133 calories	32 g carbohydrate	1 g fat
5 g fiber	2 g protein	

1 cup fresh or frozen durian	Meat of 1 young coconut
Water of 2 young coconuts	2 cups fresh spinach

1. In a high-speed blender, combine durian, coconut water, coconut meat, and spinach.

2. Blend until completely smooth.

Variation: Blackberries certainly aren't native to Indonesia, but they have a wonderful flavor affinity with durian! Try replacing young coconut in this recipe with 2 cups fresh or frozen blackberries and ½ cup water.

BLENDER BLUNDER

If you're unfamiliar with durian, you may want to try it a few times before making this smoothie. Durian is a very pungent-smelling fruit and starts to develop a more sulfurous smell and onionlike taste as it ripens. Try purchasing packaged durian to ensure you get a perfectly ripe fruit and to spare you the effort of removing the fruit from its thorny husk. Durian is a delicacy worthy of its nickname, "king of fruits," but it's unlike any other food you've ever tasted, so do a taste test before trying this tropical fruit heavyweight.

acai   The small, deep purple, phytonutrient-rich berry of the *Euterpe oleracea* palm tree, a native to the Amazon region in South America. It's well known for its high antioxidant content and is used in smoothies and juices and as a blend served with granola.

adaptogen   A plant food or herb used to rejuvenate the body. It's also said to reduce the effects of stress, anxiety, and trauma on the body.

AFA (aphanizomenon flos-aquae) blue-green algae   A cyano-bacteria commonly known as a blue-green algae. It's a high-quality source of amino acids, phycocyanin, phenylethylamine, polysaccha-rides, essential fatty acids such as EPA and DHA, and nearly every necessary vitamin and mineral.

alkalinity   Refers to a pH that's greater than 7, which is neutral. In this book, alkalinity refers to the pH of human blood in particu-lar. The proper pH for human blood is between 7.2 and 7.8, which is slightly alkaline.

aloe vera   A succulent plant, actually in the lily family, whose clear inner leaf is commonly used as a folk remedy for treating external wounds and burns and a variety of digestive and degenerative diseases.

amino acid   Small chains of molecules that form the basis of pro-teins. There are 22 standard amino acids the body utilizes, and of these, 8 appear to not be synthesized by the body and should be supplied by the diet.

anthocyanin A plant phenol that produces red, purple, and blue pigments in plants. Acai, blueberry, cranberry, and concord grapes are rich sources of this antioxidant-rich flavonoid that's said to protect against cancer, inflammation, infection, diabetes, and degenerative neurological diseases.

antioxidant Molecules that inhibit oxidation. Oxidation of molecules in the body produces free radicals that damage or kill cells. Antioxidants keep cell death in check and prevent accelerated aging.

apricot kernel The small, almondlike seed inside the apricot pit. Its flavor is stronger than almond and tastes similar to marzipan. Apricot kernels contain amygdalin and vitamin B_{17}, which is controversially disputed as either having cyanide-like toxicity to the body or as a compound that targets and kills cancer cells.

ashwagandha A small berry of the Indian *Withania somnifera* shrub said to have adaptogenic properties similar to ginseng.

bee pollen The granular beads of pollen collected by bees from a variety of plants. It's a concentrated source of vitamins, minerals, amino acids, and enzymes. It has some disputed therapeutic uses; however, if you have a severe pollen or bee allergy, consult a doctor prior to consumption.

Brazil nut The large seed kernel of the South American *Berthollrtia excelsa* tree. This nut belongs to the same family as the blueberry, cranberry, kiwi, and persimmon. They are 18 percent protein by weight and are a good source of vitamin E, calcium, magnesium, manganese, and selenium.

Brazil nut protein powder The low-fat, protein-rich by-product left after pressing the oil out of the whole Brazil nut. With the oil removed, the fiber and protein pulp are dried and ground into a powder and used for consumption.

cacao powder (raw) The material left after cold-pressing the Theobroma cacao seed for its rich oil, cacao butter. It's similar to cocoa powder but is less processed, leaving its bioactive compounds intact, and does not contain alkali. Cacao powder may be used in place of cocoa powder in smoothies or in the creation of raw chocolates.

camu camu berry The small, purple-skinned, yellow-fleshed berry of the *Myrciaria dubia* bush that grows in South America. It's currently the most concentrated known plant source of vitamin C and contains a host of phytonutrients associated with immune system support and mood enhancement.

cellulose A fibrous polysaccharide that provides structural support to the cell walls of plants. While it's the most abundant organic compound in the world, it is lacking in the modern diet, where it stimulates peristalsis and normal bowel function.

Celtic sea salt An unrefined salt product that contains 82 minerals and trace minerals as opposed to table salt, which is comprised of only 1 mineral. It serves as a source of electrolytes and does not contribute to unhealthy levels of sodium in the blood because it's not concentrated in the same way as table salt.

chai A term that literally means "tea" in many Asian languages, it also commonly refers to a spiced tea mix made with any of several warming spices such as cinnamon, clove, cardamom, ginger, black pepper, and fennel. Occasionally, rose petals, licorice root, or nutmeg may also be added.

chia seed The tiny seeds of the *Salvia hispanica*, which belongs to the mint family. Chia is a source of omega-3 fatty acids, fiber, and protein, as well as many other nutrients. They form a gel when soaked in water, which can be used as a thickening agent.

chlorella As a whole, chlorella, an algal water plant, is a concentrated source of high-quality nutrients. It's 45 percent protein and 10 percent vitamins and minerals, making it an optimal food for maintaining proper weight.

chlorophyll The phytochemical that gives plants their characteristic green color. Chlorophyll is similar in molecular structure to hemoglobin, the red pigment in human blood. It oxygenates and alkalizes the body, neutralizes bacteria, and disinfects the tissues. As a nutrient, it's rich in protein; vitamins E, C, A, and B_3; zinc; selenium; calcium; chromium; iron; magnesium; potassium; and phosphorous.

coconut oil Oil pressed from the mature seed of the *Cocos nucifera* palm tree. It's solid at room temperature and becomes liquid at 76°F. It contains medium-chain fatty acids, which are reputed to aid the breakdown of other fats in the body. It also contains lauric acid, which is only found in human breast milk.

cruciferous Plants belonging to the *Cruciferae* family. Included are vegetables of the *Brassica* genus, including broccoli, mustard, bok choy, cauliflower, and cabbage, among others.

detoxification The natural or accelerated process by which the body removes toxic substances in an effort to reach homeostasis.

digestive enzyme A type of protein that catalyzes the breakdown of food particles into a size that can be absorbed and utilized by the body.

dulse A purple-colored red algae commonly referred to as a seaweed. It contains all necessary trace minerals and is a complete protein source.

Echinacea purpurea **and** *augustifolia* The most commonly used species of this immune-stimulating plant. While there's clinical debate over echinacea's effectiveness in the prevention of or quickened recovery from illness, much folk medicine and literature supports the claim. Its immune-stimulating properties are attributed to its high phenolic content.

electrolyte Substances that have free mineral salt ions that support the electric conductivity of the nervous system. Popularized by sports drinks, electrolytes are found in abundance in fruits, vegetables, and greens.

excitotoxin Substances such as glutamate that overstimulate the neurotransmitters in the brain to the point of cell death and degenerative disease.

flaxseed oil The omega-3– and lignan-rich oil pressed from the small shiny seed of the *Linium usitatissimum*. The oil is reputed to be helpful for a number of skin maladies. It also helps prevent sunburn when consumed regularly on an empty stomach.

ginseng   An adaptogenic herb generally prepared from the dried and powdered root of the *Panax ginseng* plant. Another tonic herbal product can be produced from the dried flowers of the plant as well. Ginseng's effects are more potent when used as a synergistic herb rather than used alone.

globular protein   Water-soluble and easily digested forms of protein.

gluten   A protein composition that's difficult to digest due to its structure and causes sensitivities or allergies to wheat and other cereal grains that contain it. Gluten intolerance is a possible source of many disease issues.

goji berry   The small orange-red nightshade berry, *Lycium barbarum*, related to the wolfberry, *Lycium longum*. The berry is native to Tibet, is a source of complete protein, and is very high in vitamin A, among others. Goji berries are reputed to enhance the human life span and improve vision.

golden berry   Also commonly known as Incan berries, these are the fruit of the *Physalis peruviana* plant, native to South America. It's a larger-size gooseberry that's yellow-orange in color and grows inside a "paper lantern" similar to a tomatillo. It contains all the essential amino acids and has anti-inflammatory properties due to its content of polyphenols.

hemp protein powder   The by-product of pressing the hemp seed for its oil. Hemp protein powder is about 66 percent easily digested and absorbed protein and has the added benefit of being accompanied by plant fiber.

hemp seed   The tiny seeds of the *Cannabis sativa* plant. They're free of any THC content and are a complete protein source that also provides fiber, chlorophyll, omega fatty acids, most vitamins, and nearly all minerals.

high-speed blender   A blender with higher voltage and Hz than a traditional blender. It has the capacity to powder nuts, crush ice, and reduce nearly any vegetable, fruit, or green to a creamy silky texture. It's an essential tool for producing blended foods with optimized nutrition.

Himalayan crystal salt A crystalline form of salt mined in Pakistan. It derives its pink color from iron oxide and is said to contain 82 other minerals.

hydrochloric acid The main component of gastric fluid. It denatures proteins into a form that makes them easily broken down by digestive enzymes.

Incan berry *See* golden berry.

jamu An herbal drink used in Indonesia as a folk medicine. Ingredients in jamu vary greatly but usually contain ginger and turmeric, among many others.

jing A term in traditional Chinese medicine that refers to life force within the human body. Every person has *jing* that's inborn and cannot be replenished, as well as acquired *jing*, which improves longevity by protecting stores of inborn *jing*.

lamb's quarters A common edible weed, *Chenopodium berlandieri*, nutritionally similar to spinach.

lassi A yogurt-based Indian drink. It may be served as a savory herbal drink or as a sweet drink, but it's most well known for the mango lassi variation.

lemongrass Common and widely used lemongrass, *Cymbopogon citratus* is a cultivated reed plant that imparts its distinctive flavors into well-known dishes such as Thai curries. It has anti-carcinogenic properties that are helpful as a killer of cancer cells.

lychee Fruits come from the *Litchi chinensis* tree native to Southern China and Southeast Asia. The white, juicy fruit has a grapelike flavor that's fragrant and floral tasting. It's covered by a thin, easily peeled skin and reveals a somewhat large, shiny brown seed when the fruit is removed.

maca (*Lepidium meyenii*) A protein-rich root from South America that's eaten as a vegetable, similar to potatoes. Maca offers non-specific support to the endocrine system and tones the adrenals.

macronutrients Nutrients that provide caloric value such as carbohydrates, fats, and proteins.

mangosteen   The small, white-fleshed fruit of the *Garcinia mangostana* tree native to Indonesia. The fruit is contained inside a hard and thick purple rind and contains edible seeds. While the fruit portion of the plant is used for various folk remedies, it's the deep purple rind that gives mangosteen products their purple color and phytonutrient value.

maqui berry   A berry with a black-purple color indicating its high anthocyanin content. Its impressive antioxidant content is reputed with anti-aging effects and is also said to fight fatigue.

matcha   The dried and powdered leaf of the *Camellia sinensis*, green tea plant. In addition to the antioxidants provided by green tea, matcha also contains chlorophyll not present in prepared green tea.

mesquite pod meal   A mineral-rich edible pod fruit related to carob. It carries similar health benefits to carob, including blood sugar modulation.

metabolic enzyme   A protein that catalyzes chemical reactions that take place within and between cells. Our bodies are completely dependent upon them for all necessary life functions.

micronutrient   Nutrients that include vitamins, minerals, enzymes, and phytonutrients.

nettle   The stinging nettle, which is botanically *Urtica dioica*. Nettles have a diuretic effect helpful for the kidneys and also aid arthritis and anemia. They grow throughout North America and should be handled with care to avoid being stung.

nopal cactus   A cactus that yields flat, fleshy leaves and pear-shape fruits.

omega-3 fatty acid   A class of fatty acids necessary for proper brain function.

organosulfurs   A class of phytonutrients that occur in shiitake mushrooms and garlic. Many of these compounds have tumor-fighting properties.

oxytocin   A hormone that plays an important role in bonding. Chocolate is a plant source of oxytocin.

pea protein   The protein portion separated from the carbohydrate portion of the yellow split pea.

pectin   A fiber found in citrus fruits.

peristalsis   The natural, wavelike movement of the smooth muscles of the digestive tract. This movement pushes food through the digestive tract as it's broken down and eliminates waste from the colon.

pH   Refers to the chemical balance of a solution. Water is neutral at 7 pH, while basic solutions have a pH higher than 7 and acidic solutions have a pH lower than 7. The ideal pH for human blood is between 7.2 and 7.8, which is slightly basic.

phenols   Bioactive phytonutrients found in berries, chocolate, olives, and many fruits and vegetables. Certain plant phenols have been found to inhibit tumors and have useful antimicrobial, anti-inflammatory, and antiviral properties.

phenylethylamine   A neurotransmitter that alleviates depression and contributes to feelings of well-being.

phytonutrient   The bioactive compounds in plants that produce distinctive smells, colors, and flavors. They often play a key role in health maintenance and healing.

pine pollen   A bioactive source of essential amino acids, vitamins, minerals, and other health-giving components. It's said to impart strength and virility to those who consume it. Pine pollen in particular is hand-harvested from the pine cones of various pine trees and is a vegan product.

polysaccharide   A part of the carbohydrate group that includes fibers such as cellulose and pectin. It also includes beta-glucans, which activate the immune system.

prickly pear   The green or red fruit from the nopal cactus. The spines and skin must be removed before consumption. The inner flesh and seeds are edible.

reishi mushroom (*Ganoderma lucidum*)   A mushroom with almost supernatural powers of health and healing. It contains terpenes and polysaccharides that make it useful in treating cancer and autoimmune diseases. It's bitter tasting, and the powdered mushroom may be easily mixed into other foods to mask the flavor.

rice protein   The protein portion of the rice grain that's been enzymatically separated from the carbohydrate portion of the rice grain. It's easily digested and is a healthy alternative to whey-based protein.

rooibos   Afrikaans for "red bush," *Aspalathus linearis*, it's a member of the legume family, although the part used is the leaf. The red color is imparted by a fermentation process that turns the leaves from green to red. Rooibos is antioxidant and antifungal.

rose water   A highly scented water produced from the distillation of rose petals.

shen   A term used in Chinese medicine to describe the reservoir of energy one has. It may either refer to acquired *shen* or to the finite amount of *shen* one is born with. It's thought that when the unreplenishable inborn *shen* is exhausted, life ends.

sorrel   A wild green, often referred to as a weed, that has a sour flavor and may be used in ways similar to spinach. There are many subspecies, but common sorrel has leaves shaped somewhat like arrows and resembles spinach.

spirulina   Generally either refers to the *cyanobacteria Arthrospira plantensis* or to *Arthrospira maxima*. Spirulina is a source of easily assimilated protein, omega fatty acids, and a host of vitamins and minerals.

standard American diet (SAD)   The modern Western diet of processed foods, large amounts of dairy, rich meats, fried foods or foods with hydrogenated oils, and excess sugar, which offers little actual nutritional value. It's largely devoid of fresh fruits and vegetables, and fosters disease rather than health.

superfood   Foods that represent sources of concentrated nutrition. Most superfoods also contain high levels of phytochemicals that give them healing or medicinal properties.

tahini   The seed butter or paste made from ground sesame seeds. It's a commonly used ingredient in Middle Eastern cuisine.

tamarind   The *Tamarindus indica* tree bears a sweet, tart, chewy fruit inside a thin-shelled pod. Its flavor is similar to a sour raisin with a datelike texture.

terpenes   A class of polyphenols, which are the active compounds that give plants their distinctive scents. Essential oils are mostly made up of various essential oils. Carotenoids and quercitin are examples of nutritious terpenes.

Thai basil (*Ocimum basilicum*)   A sweet basil that has a distinctively different flavor from that of common basil that holds up better when cooked. It's a frequent ingredient in Asian cuisine.

tonic   As referred to in this book, a tonic is an herbal substance that promotes general health or invigorates particular organs in the body.

trace mineral   Minerals required by the body in very minute amounts. These are minerals such as manganese and selenium as opposed to calcium and potassium, which the body needs in larger amounts.

turmeric   A spice used in Indian, Asian, and Middle Eastern cuisine. The part used is the bright yellow-orange root of the *Curcuma longa* plant, which is a member of the ginger family. Turmeric may be used fresh or dried and powdered in a variety of dishes. Turmeric has traditionally been used as an anti-inflammatory, antiseptic ingredient and has reputed uses as a treatment for cancer as well as several other diseases, which are currently under research.

wheatgrass juice   The pressed juice of the wheat berry sprout, *Triticum aestivum*. Wheatgrass is reputed with being an effective treatment for diabetes, hypertension, and cancer. It chelates heavy metals and has superb nutritional qualities that correct many deficiencies.

young coconut   An immature or "green" coconut that contains a sweet liquid and a soft gelatinous meat rather than a hard, fibrous, oily meat. They are often left with some of the white husk remaining and appear in markets as white, cylindrical cones.

Resources

In this appendix, I've compiled resources and support for those of you wishing to explore the role of green smoothies as an integral part of a healthy lifestyle and its affect on health and healing. You'll find online sources for exotic or hard-to-find ingredients as well as myriad books and websites full of relevant health information.

Books About Green Smoothies

Boutenko, Victoria. *Green for Life*. Ashland, OR: Raw Family Publishing, 2005.

———. *Green Smoothie Revolution: The Radical Leap Towards Natural Health*. Berkeley, CA: North Atlantic Books, 2009.

Caldwell, Kim. *How Green Smoothies Saved My Life*. Cordova, TN: Together Publishing, 2009.

Openshaw, Robyn. *Green Smoothies Diet: The Natural Program for Extraordinary Health*. Berkeley, CA: Ulysses Press, 2009.

Books to Support a Healthy Lifestyle

Burroughs, Stanley. *The Master Cleanser*. Reno, NV: Burroughs Books, 1976.

Campbell, Colin T., and Thomas M. Campbell II. *The China Study: The Most Comprehensive Study of Nutrition Ever Conducted and the Startling Implications for Diet, Weight Loss, and Long-Term Health*. Dallas, TX: Benbella Books, 2006.

Cousens, Gabriel. *Conscious Eating.* Berkeley, CA: North Atlantic Books, 2000.

———. *Rainbow Green Live Food Cuisine.* Berkeley, CA: North Atlantic Books, 2003.

———. *Spiritual Nutrition: Six Foundations for Spiritual Life and the Awakening of Kundalini.* Berkeley, CA: North Atlantic Books, 2005.

Elias, Thomas S., and Peter A. Dykeman. *Edible Wild Plants: A North American Field Guide.* New York, NY: Sterling Publishing Company, 1990.

Esselstyn, Caldwell. *Prevent and Reverse Heart Disease.* New York, NY: Avery, 2007.

Graham, Dr. Douglas N. *The 80/10/10 Diet.* Key Largo, FL: FoodnSport Press, 2006.

Klein, David. *Self Healing Colitis and Crohn's.* Sebastopol, CA: Colitis and Crohn's Health Recovery Center, 2006.

Kulvinskas, Victoras. *Survival into the 21st Century: Planetary Healers Manual.* Woodstock Valley, CT: 21st Century Publications, 1981.

Marcus, Erik. *Vegan: The New Ethics of Eating.* Ithaca, NY: McBooks Press, 2001.

McLaughlin, Chris. *The Complete Idiot's Guide to Small-Space Gardening.* Indianapolis, IN: Alpha Books, 2012.

Ornish, Dean. *Dr. Ornish's Program for Reversing Heart Disease: The Only System Scientifically Proven to Reverse Heart Disease Without Drugs or Surgery.* New York, NY: Ivy Books, 1995.

Price Bowman, Daria, and Carl A. Price. *The Complete Idiot's Guide to Edible Gardening.* Indianapolis, IN: Alpha Books, 2003.

Reinfeld, Mark, and Bo Rinaldi. *The Complete Idiot's Guide to Eating Raw.* Indianapolis, IN: Alpha Books, 2008.

———. *Vegan Fusion World Cuisine: Extraordinary Recipes and Timeless Wisdom from the Celebrated Blossoming Lotus Restaurants.* New York, NY: Beaufort Books, 2007.

Robbins, John. *Diet for a New America*. Tiburon, CA: HJ Kramer, 1987.

Wigmore, Ann. *The Hippocrates Diet and Health Program*. New York, NY: Avery, 1983.

Sources for Herbs and Superfood Ingredients

The Raw Food World

rawfoodworld.com

The Raw Food World is the one-stop shop for superfoods, herbs, information, and equipment pertaining to healing with whole plant foods.

Golden Lotus Botanicals

goldenlotusherbs.com

This webstore contains a comprehensive apothecary of herbs and other tonics from traditional Chinese medicine, the Amazon, India, and Western traditions.

Blue Mountain Organics

bluemountainorganics.com

This online store carries a line of sprouted organic nut and seed butters from Better Than Roasted brand. These are the highest-quality nut butters on the market and are highly recommended over traditional nut butters. Check out their other raw and superfood products as well.

Really Wild Food Guide

countrylovers.co.uk/wildfoodjj/weedgall.htm

This is a great resource for identifying edible plants that may be growing near you. Check out the illustrated list of edible greens and flowers.

Rejuvenative Foods

rejuvenative.com

Go here for any type of raw organic nut or seed butter you can think of. They're fresh and guaranteed not to be rancid. They also sell cultured vegetables.

Earth Circle Organics

earthcircleorganics.com

Find wholesale nuts, dried fruits, raw oils, and superfoods here at reasonable prices.

High Vibe

highvibe.com

This site offers an online store, recipes, fasting information, testimonials, interviews, and much more.

Lifestyle Management Support

Vegan Fusion Cuisine

veganfusion.com

This is the website my *Complete Idiot's Guide to Eating Raw* co-author Mark Reinfeld and I host. It contains links to our informative newsletter and *7 Minute Chef* ebook. Be sure to sign up to receive free recipes, the latest news, and updates on Blossoming Lotus Restaurants.

Cooking Healthy Lessons

cookinghealthylessons.com

This is another of our websites, which provides access to a wealth of vegan cooking lessons; cutting-edge health research; and an ever-growing number of informative, life-affirming, and inspiring ebooks. Be sure to sign up to receive all these indispensible tools for healthy vegan living!

Green Smoothie Challenge

greensmoothiechallenge.com

This website offers the perfect support program to beginning your green smoothie journey. It focuses on cleansing and healing smoothies and recommends a 14-day program to get your digestion on track.

TeraWarner.com

terawarner.com

Team up with health experts in the field of detoxifying the natural way! This blog provides support programs for cleansing with green smoothies.

Smoothie Handbook
smoothie-handbook.com
This website is all about smoothies. It even has a section dedicated to green smoothies.

Colitis and Crohn's Health Recovery Center
colitis-crohns.com
This site is an indispensible resource for anyone suffering from digestive disorders such as irritable bowel syndrome (IBS), colitis, or Crohn's disease. Learn about self-healing with whole foods.

RawReform.com
rawreform.com
Angela Stokes is a remarkable young woman who recovered from morbid obesity by adopting a raw food diet. Her testimonial, ebooks, online store, before and after pictures, and links to interviews are all available on this site. She's a strong proponent of green smoothies and regularly hosts and assists online support groups for green smoothie fasts.

Tree of Life
gabrielcousens.com
Raw food guru Dr. Gabriel Cousens started the Tree of Life Rejuvenation Center in Patagonia, Arizona. The center offers nightly rates, detox/cleansing packages, workshops, a live food café, apprenticeships, nutrition programs, and an online store.

Hippocrates Health Institute
hippocratesinst.com
The Hippocrates Health Institute, founded by Ann Wigmore in West Palm Beach, Florida, offers a 1- to 3-week program teaching the Hippocrates lifestyle. The center was named the number-one teaching institute by Spa Management Group in 2000.

Optimum Health Institute
optimumhealth.org
The Optimum Health Institute, located in San Diego, California, and Austin, Texas, offers programs in ancient spiritual disciplines to promote healing. It's run by a nondenominational church that aims to heal people by cleansing the body, mind, and spirit.

Gerson Institute
gerson.org
The Gerson Institute, founded by Max Gerson's daughter, Charlotte, is a nonprofit organization committed to the nontoxic treatment of disease. This institute refers people to licensed Gerson clinics and practitioners.

Raw Family
rawfamily.com
Victoria Boutenko, author of *Green for Life* and *The Green Smoothie Revolution*, shares her experiences of healing her entire family with green smoothies and a raw diet.

The Garden Diet
thegardendiet.com
This family-friendly site offers support and advice from long-time health pioneers and raw foodists Storm and Jinjee, who have raised their entire family on raw food.

HappyCow
happycow.net
HappyCow is the most comprehensive global vegetarian dining guide and directory of natural health food stores on the web. It's a great resource for those wishing to find healthy raw or vegan-friendly restaurants and stores while traveling.

The Eat Local Challenge
eatlocal.net
Find information and resources about eating locally in your area here.

Vitamix
vitamix.com
Find the latest Vitamix blenders here on the official site, including factory-reconditioned models for less that still come with a 7-year warranty. For free shipping in the continental United States, enter coupon code 06-002510.

Index

H

Q–R

S

T